The Long Table

MY LOVE AFFAIR WITH FOOD

To my mother Muriel - a loving cook with a light hand.

The Long Table

MY LOVE AFFAIR WITH FOOD

MARY MOODY

Contents

It would seem

that families are divided into two distinct groups. Those for whom food and shared family meals are essential to their way of life; and those for whom food is merely the fuel that keeps them going from one day to the next.

I belong to the first group, and have done all my life. I was born into a turbulent family but my childhood was punctuated by discussions about food; by menu planning, by recipe hunting followed by adventurous shopping, shared cooking and rapturous eating.

My father was unusual for his time – a man who loved to cook, although I assume this practical talent was prompted by the tragic death of his first wife and a need to develop survival skills for his young family – my half brother and sister. My mother, when she married my father, couldn't boil an egg. She quickly learned, and became one of the most sublime cooks I have ever known. My parents' friends were writers, journalists and political activists. Although our home life was often fraught with domestic tensions it was also a stimulating and fascinating environment for a child, full of lively conversations and heated debates. Food was always part of the equation.

Mum was time poor because she went back to work when I was seven years old and she naturally involved me in helping around the kitchen. By the time I was ten

I was quite capable of preparing and serving a simple family meal and I derived great satisfaction from this task. Although I didn't realise it at the time, the cooking of food to share has always been for me an act of love. Probably the most basic act of love there is. While some people regard cooking as a 'chore', for me, from the very beginning it was all about giving pleasure and, in turn, receiving praise and approbation.

I sometimes ponder on how many mouths I have fed over these last forty (or more) years. As a teenager in a share house I did most of the cooking, and although there were only six of us the numbers at dinnertime were often twice that. When I met my husband David 36 years ago I seduced him not just with my ready smile and sense of humour, but my much-practiced repertoire of family recipes. As a young mother I loved watching my growing children respond positively to good food and couldn't wait to introduce them to new and different tastes. It seemed natural that making delicious meals was a vital part of nurturing my family.

For decades when we lived in the Blue Mountains west of Sydney, I routinely cooked dinner for seven every night of the week; my mother (who lived with us for 25 years after the death of my father), my husband and our four children. Though we didn't have much money in those early years, our table was always laden with good food. Eventually, when we could afford it, we had a table made that could accommodate not just our own family, but friends and their children as well. This was the long table. Made from Australian hardwood it seats 16 comfortably – 18 at a pinch – with benches instead of chairs so that the smaller children can be squashed down one end together. For most of this time I cooked on a wood-burning fuel stove – a wonderful Rayburn – keeping the large kitchen where the table was positioned cosy and filled with the rich aromas of whatever was simmering on the hob or roasting in the oven.

Indeed, my passion for food turned me into a gardener. In the 1970s I read about the overload of chemicals in the food chain and decided to grow my own organic vegetables, herbs and fruit and keep my own free-range chickens. This environmental decision ironically created a career for me – I became a gardening writer, using my skills as a journalist to describe my journey of discovery as an organic gardener.

When our children were teenagers our house became a refuge for their dread-locked, bare-footed friends who came to visit and to eat with us, often staying for days or weeks at a time. 'Don't you have a home to go to?' David would sometimes ask in exasperation. And they would drift off for a day or two, only to return to the warmth of the kitchen and the welcome offered by the long table. Friends and colleagues came too – actors, writers, journalists, photographers, filmmakers and activists involved in local politics. Just as my parents had done, we revelled in the company of like-minded people and passionate, often high-spirited conversation. It all took place around the table.

These days the table sits empty for much of the time because the children have grown and left home and it's just David and me rattling around a big old house together. We now live on a farm where I can garden to my heart's content and harvest even more fresh produce to bring to the pantry and table. We get together as often as we can – four adult children and their partners plus eight grandchildren – and when we do, the table is overflowing once more with the same atmosphere that I love so much: intense conversation, hilarious laughter and the sheer delight of sharing a meal together. Our grandchildren have inherited our passion for food and delight in coming with me to the garden to pick ingredients for our lunch; love planning what we will eat for dinner; love helping (the older ones) prepare a meal or set the table. And the only time they are quiet is those first few minutes when the food is put in front of them. It's the most satisfying silence of all.

adly made porridge is lumpy and
should be rich, smooth and satis
icky washing up of the saucepan
ftermath is far less messy.

Perfect porridge (recipe p29)

Gr

nappea

ing. Pe

ut if yo

well

the

the

owing up

Of all the senses, smell is the most evocative. To this day if I am cooking a 'baked dinner' I can close my eyes and instantly be back in my childhood home on a Sunday morning, especially if Beethoven is playing because that was our weekly ritual. Classical music on the radio and a roast every Sunday lunchtime – spring, summer, autumn and winter. My mother smoked and did the ironing, damping down my father's starched white shirts while sipping on a tumbler of sweet sherry. My father did the cooking.

We lived in a two-storey block of flats overlooking Sydney's glorious Balmoral Beach and my bedroom was a glassed-in veranda with spectacular views through the harbour headlands. These days it's millionaire's row, but in the 1950s it was middle class – the North Shore hadn't established its identity and the wealthy seldom ventured over the Harbour Bridge.

My parents were both journalists and they met and fell in love while working for the *Daily Telegraph* newspaper in 1941. Theo was a widower with two young children and Muriel was only 21, painfully thin with wild black hair and brilliant blue eyes. He was the news editor and she was a nervous young court reporter, and one of the fastest shorthand writers in the business. They married and shortly afterwards my father left for America as the *Telegraph's* US wartime correspondent. My mother was left behind with the children to care for and it was six months before she managed to get passage on a ship so that the three of them could join him in New York.

Balmoral

PACIFIC OCEAN→

NORTH SYDNEY

Sydney Harbour Bridge

SYDNEY HARBOUR

SYDNEY

The Long Table

My parents in Sydney in 1941 where they met and fell in love while both were working for the *Daily Telegraph* newspaper.

Me as a freckle-faced beach girl. The Australian sun didn't suit my Irish red hair and pale skin.

The Spode china, 'Chinese Rose', which my father bought for Mum after the War.

Every time I dust flour on my mother's old wooden rolling pin, memories of her came flooding back.

Old family china is used and not just left getting dusty in a cupboard.

My brother Jon and sister Margaret with my mother Muriel on a street corner in New York during the War. The years spent in America had a profound impact.

Mum was a great storyteller, and her reminiscences of their adventures overseas were filled with hilarious anecdotes and details about every aspect of their daily lives. It was true that she couldn't cook when she met Dad and he taught her the basics, sometimes phoning with step-by-step instructions from his newspaper office in Manhattan. I loved the story about her making pea and ham soup for the first time. Under strict instructions she boiled the green split peas with a smoked ham bone, onions, carrots, potatoes and bay leaf. When it was cooked she phoned Dad at work for further directions.

'Remove the ham bone then strain the soup over the sink. Put the peas and vegetables through a sieve and add this to the strained liquid,' he told her.

She did exactly as she was told, only he had neglected to tell her that she would need to put a large saucepan in the sink first to catch the liquid as it was being strained. Most of the soup ended up down the drain and he was not amused!

After the War when the family returned to Sydney, Mum brought back her copper-bottomed stainless steel saucepans and heavy cast iron skillets, which I still use to this day. She also carried a copy of the classic American food bible – *The Joy of Cooking* by Marion Rombauer Becker, which she thumbed until it fell apart in the late 1950s. Luckily she managed to find another edition, which I have on my kitchen shelf and use constantly, especially when making desserts for family gatherings. When I flick through the book I

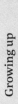

Growing up

15

Mum kept the first shoes worn by my brother Danny and me; she was always sentimental.

She used her American stainless steel pots and pans until the day she died.

I feel a sense of continuity and connection to the past.

As a teenager in the 1960s with my niece Louise, the daughter of my brother Jon.

Mum wasn't into gadgets but she used this one for chopping parsley. It was tricky to clean afterwards!

As a child I felt well-loved despite the domestic upheavals.

Brother Danny with blond curls and me minus hair and teeth in an old-fashioned cane pram.

The tradition of a Sunday roast at lunchtime has been maintained, and is especially enjoyed by my grandchildren, still served on their great-grandmother Muriel's china.

My mother was an affectionate woman who constantly hugged us and told us we were special.

My mother with her own mother, Ellen Angel, who I met when I was a toddler but sadly don't remember.

My mother's cookbooks were in constant use and she tucked recipes torn from magazines between the pages and wrote her own recipes on the inside covers.

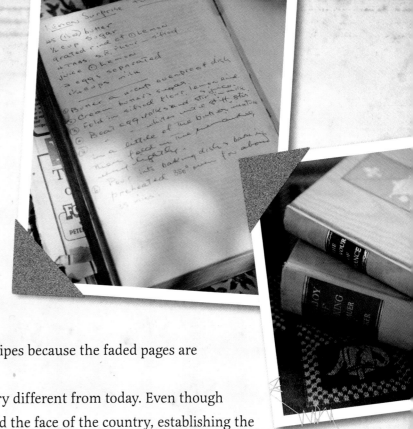

can easily recognise my mother's favourite recipes because the faded pages are food-splattered from frequent use.

In 1950s Australia the cuisine was very different from today. Even though European migration after the War had changed the face of the country, establishing the beginnings of multiculturalism, it took more than a decade for our taste in food to change accordingly. Most Australians ate very simple meals, based on the English tradition. Grilled or roasted meats and baked or mashed potatoes served with carrots, beans, peas, cauliflower or cabbage. There were no zucchinis or eggplants, virtually no pasta (apart from tinned spaghetti), only the blandest of salamis, and garlic was considered beneath contempt (the smell oozed from the bodies of people who ate it). Wine was only served on special occasions – most Australians simply weren't familiar with the taste of it. People made soups and simple stews of lamb or beef and for a change there was corned beef and cabbage or shepherd's pie. Chicken was very expensive and usually served only as a Christmas treat because turkey wasn't fashionable or readily available. 'Pudding' was popular back then – apple pies, stewed fruit and prunes and custards with healthy options like sago and tapioca. It was a limited and predictable cuisine – indeed I have one friend who said that in her household they ate grilled lamp chops, mashed potatoes, boiled carrots and peas every night of the week except Friday when they ate fish pie.

There were very few restaurants in Australia during this period. In the city there were some smart establishments for businessmen's lunches and a few snazzy nightclubs. Apart from that it was Greek milkbars and Chinese restaurants in the suburbs and in every country town. People just didn't 'eat out' in those days and there was no such thing as take-away except for fish and chips or a meat pie from the local bakery. People shopped for basic raw ingredients then cooked their meals from scratch.

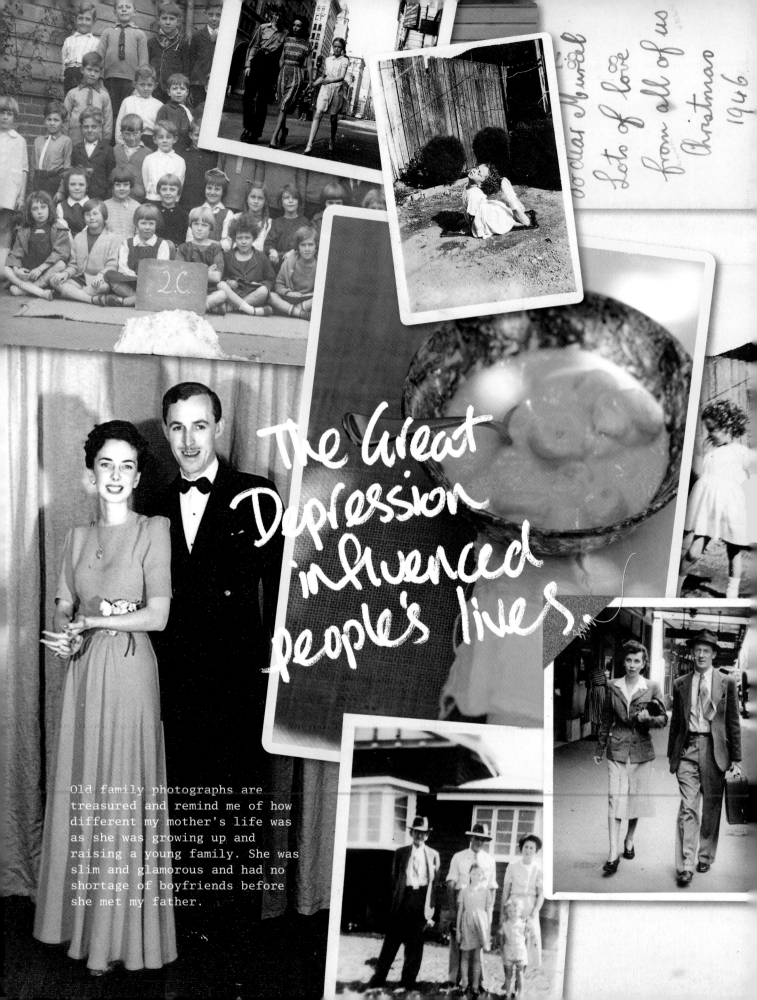

The Great Depression influenced people's lives.

Lots of love from all of us Christmas 1946

Old family photographs are treasured and remind me of how different my mother's life was as she was growing up and raising a young family. She was slim and glamorous and had no shortage of boyfriends before she met my father.

Mum trained in classical ballet
from early childhood and dreamt
of dancing professionally until
her father died and she was
required to leave school and
work to help support her mother.

The way we shopped was very different then too. I remember the first small supermarket opening in Mosman in the 1960s, but before that it was the grocer, the butcher, the greengrocer and the fish shop. For many years we had no car – Mum would catch the tram to the junction, drop off her hand-written lists at the various shops then take a walk down hill to home. By late afternoon neatly packed cartons would arrive on the back doorstep. Simple as that. Even the diced kangaroo meat we fed our cats was delivered twice a week by the local pet shop. Milk was delivered in glass bottles every morning and freshly baked bread was also slipped into our 'servery' door three times a week. In those days milk was milk, butter was butter and flour was flour. There were no choices. No skim or Vitamin D added or unsalted or gluten free. I must confess when I stand gazing in a befuddled fashion at the vast array of choices on a modern supermarket shelf I often yearn for a return to those uncomplicated days.

Our kitchen in the flat was very small indeed. Nothing more than a narrow corridor between a pebbled concrete bench that contained the kitchen sink and, on the other side, a shallow pantry cupboard. There was a gas stove at one end and a small refrigerator near the back door. There was no room for more than one person in the kitchen at any time and it's amazing how so many excellent meals were produced from such an inadequate space. There were no labour-saving devices or fancy gadgets. Wooden spoons, a hand beater for whipping cream and a wall-mounted can opener were about as high-tech as it came!

My mother was not a born housekeeper. She cheerfully washed our clothes – for many years in an old copper before being given a washing machine and wringer – and she didn't object to ironing. She loved to cook – and she was very good at it – but all other aspects of domestic organisation eluded her. The kitchen cupboards were a chaotic jumble

Hot and happy summer days at Balmoral Beach.

Mum and me.

In the 1950s we were healthy with lots of walking and swimming and a diet based on fresh ingredients and home-cooking. Life was less complicated then, although not necessarily happier.

Our first school was Balmoral Infants, overlooking the beach where Danny and I spent many hours getting sunburnt at weekends and school holidays. Sadly the school has disappeared and those of my friends who I still keep in touch with feel the loss as much as I do.

BALMORAL BEACH KINDER 1955

of jars and packets and condiments, the fridge was jam-packed with mysterious saucers of ancient leftovers, and in the living and dining rooms every surface was piled high with clutter. The windows would be cleaned only when visibility became impossible and I'm sure our bathtub never saw a sprinkling of Ajax. I was often embarrassed to ask friends home, and developed the bad habit (which I have never managed to shake) of sweeping clutter out of sight into drawers.

But Mum fed us lovingly, which was so much more important than polishing the sideboard. Breakfast was substantial, especially in winter. No person went out the front door on an empty stomach. We never had breakfast cereals but porridge was made every night – the oatmeal was soaked in water in a double boiler and it was then heated up slowly the following morning and served with brown sugar and cream. It's amazing that we weren't overweight when I consider what Mum cooked to follow the porridge — bacon and eggs, bubble and squeak. Sometimes she would grill leftover steak or chops and serve them with stewed tomato on toast. With a fried egg! And at the weekends there were grilled kippers or smoked cod with lashings of butter and parsley.

My Dad loved to go fishing on his days off. He would set out before dawn and sometimes allow my brother Dan or me to tag along. It was such a special treat. He caught small tailor, bream and leather jackets then cleaned and gutted them on the jetty, bringing the catch back in time for my mother to cook them for our breakfast. She simply washed and patted them dry with a tea towel, dusted them with flour, salt and pepper and fried them in butter. Heavenly!

Our school lunches were also thoughtfully prepared. No white bread, vegemite sandwiches for us. It was wholemeal or grain bread, salad and cheese or ham and often a hard-boiled egg (with salt and pepper twisted into a small square of greaseproof paper), dried fruits and nuts as well as fresh fruit. I have to confess that I sometimes swapped with my friends; my favourite being the lunch of a girl whose mother made her sandwiches of white bread and butter with a filling of green jelly crystals. Horrific!

And the reason we didn't get fat with this starchy, meat-laden diet was that we also ate masses of fresh vegetables and we walked everywhere and swam in the ocean all summer long. It was a healthy lifestyle.

I think about our childhood a
lot and most of my memories are
happy and carefree. Children
had more physical freedom
back then and were also given
greater responsibilities.

I was seven years old when Mum returned to work. When I got home from school I had a handful of 'chores', including the basic preparation of the evening meal. Peeling potatoes, top and tailing beans, shelling peas (no such thing as frozen peas), dicing carrots and placing the lamb chops under the griller. I would set the table and have everything in order for the evening meal by the time my parents arrived home at about 5.30pm. Being a helper around the house made life a little more harmonious for everyone. I realise now that I developed strategies to help keep the peace in what had become a very volatile marriage, and the role of 'smoothing troubled waters' is one that has remained with me.

Although, like most Australians, we had our fair share of grilled meat and sausages, we also ate a lot of casseroles and stews. In winter Mum would cook these at the weekend for heating up on busy weeknights. Anything that was left over was reheated and served on thick slabs of toast for breakfast. Other weeknight favourites were corned beef and cabbage and pickled pork. More fancy dinners, like homemade steak and kidney pie were cooked on Saturday night, and Sunday night was our only casual meal – grilled cheese and tomato on toast in front of the radio, then eventually in front of the television.

Friday night was also a bit more relaxed, and sometimes we would get fish and chips. Mum would never allow us to eat them out of the paper – they were served on plates around the dining table with bread and butter and a tossed salad. In mid-summer Dad would stop off at the fish shop and get a couple of pounds of prawns and several dozen oysters. We would all walk to the beach – he would carry a couple of bottles of beer and Mum the bread and butter. Nothing could be more heady and delicious that a freshly peeled prawn sandwich eaten while sitting on the rocks with feet dangling in the water.

We had two roast dinners a week – Sunday lunch and a smaller roast on Wednesday such as a shoulder of lamb or, if Dad had won at the horse races, a chicken. Dad drank wine at home, consuming copious quantities of flagon claret every week night as well as all weekend. Dad drank anything except sweet sherry which became my mother's favourite tipple. It was the only alcohol she could rest assured wouldn't be drained from the bottle in the middle of the night when Dad was on a bender. I honestly believe that the good food, the good conversation and the idyllic beach setting made for a happy childhood in spite of all the domestic traumas.

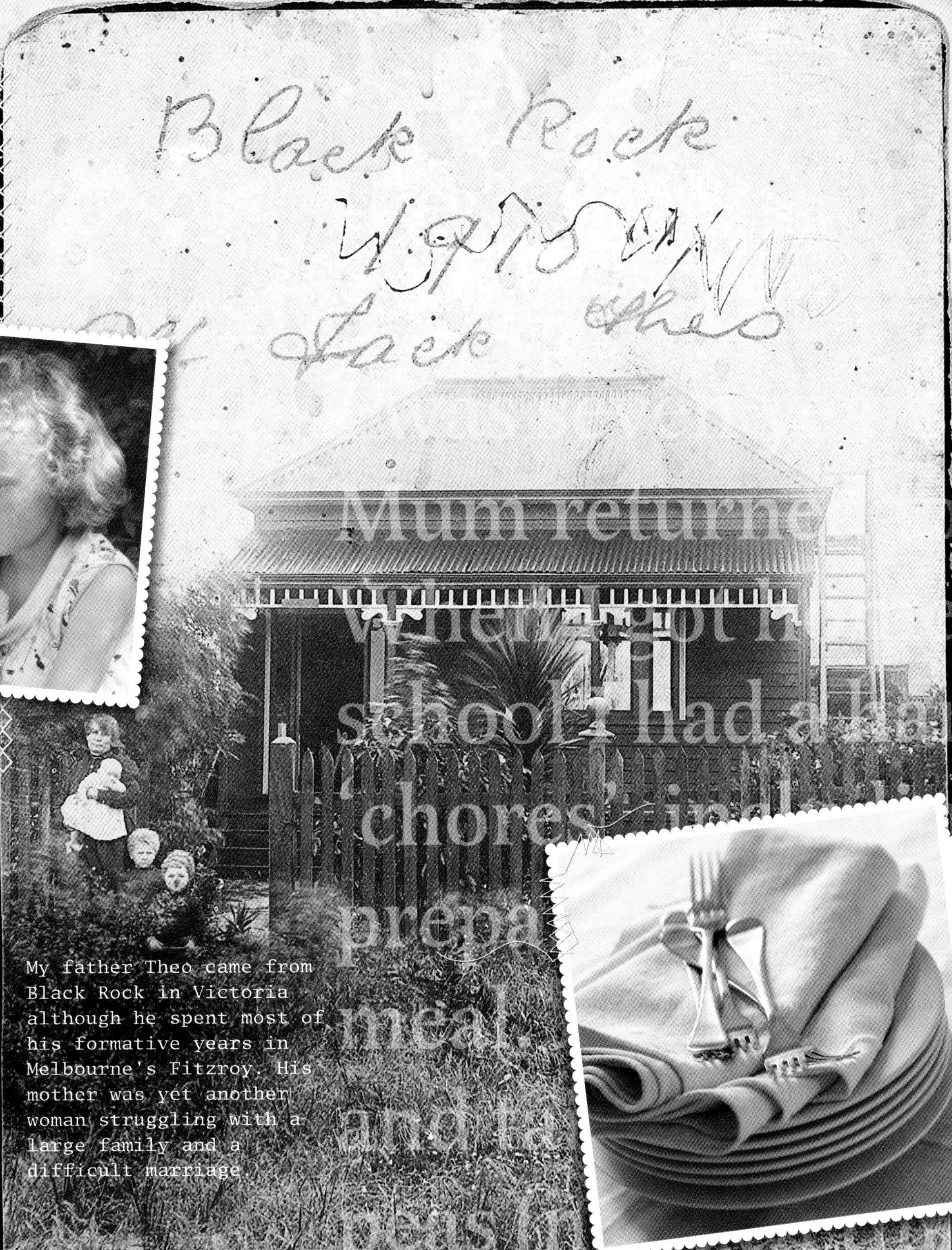

Black Rock

of Jack theo

Mum returne
when got ri
school I had a
chores i
prepa
meal
and ta
peas
frozen peas, a
and placing the la
under the grille

My father Theo came from
Black Rock in Victoria
although he spent most of
his formative years in
Melbourne's Fitzroy. His
mother was yet another
woman struggling with a
large family and a
difficult marriage

My father Theo as a very young man – always a dapper dresser and very proud of his appearance.

Smoked cod and poached eggs

Breakfast

In the 1950s our meals were much meatier and breakfast was important. During winter Mum would often cook steak or chops and eggs and use leftover vegetables to fry up bubble and squeak. Fish was also a popular breakfast food, along with eggs fried in butter. It was just as well we walked to school and back, to burn off all that fat!

Retro recipes

Perfect porridge

Badly made porridge is lumpy and unappealing – if cooked well it should be rich, smooth and satisfying. People are put off by the sticky washing up of the saucepan, but if you make it this way the aftermath is far less messy.

¾ cup of oatmeal per person
water
salt
warmed milk
1 tablespoon of brown sugar per person

Use a double boiler or if you don't have one, place an ovenproof bowl over a saucepan with 20 cm of water in the bottom. Soaking the oatmeal overnight is a great help – simply put the oatmeal into the double boiler with a pinch of salt and cover completely with water. Check before going to bed, and top up the water if it has been absorbed.
In the morning put the heat under the saucepan and let the oatmeal warm through, stirring occasionally with a wooden spoon. Add water if the porridge is too thick – the amount added will depend on the consistency you prefer. When smooth, add a couple of tablespoons of milk (or pouring cream) to make it creamier and serve in warm bowls with brown sugar and warm milk. Some members of our family prefer porridge with extra salt and cream rather than the sugar!
cooking time 15 minutes

Smoked cod and poached eggs

This orange-coloured smoked fish was very popular in the Fifties and makes a wonderful Sunday breakfast.

1 piece of smoked cod per person
2 eggs per person
½ tablespoon butter
black pepper
finely chopped parsley for serving

Use a heavy based frying pan and fill one third with lightly salted water. Heat until the water starts to simmer then slide in the fish pieces. Depending on the number of people you are cooking for, you can poach the eggs in the same water. With both the fish and the eggs, the idea if to keep the water at a slow simmer – not boiling vigorously. You can use a fork to stir the water, creating a whirlpool effect so that when you crack the egg into the water the yolk will form a neater shape.
The cod only needs to be heated – 8-10 minutes – while the eggs should only take 2-3 minutes. Remove both the fish and eggs with a slotted spoon, allowing as much water as possible to drain away before serving on warmed plates, dotted with butter and sprinkled with the parsley and black pepper.
cooking time 10 minutes

Balmoral Beach was popular but never overcrowded when we were growing up. Once we could swim safely we were set free to explore and enjoy its natural beauty.

Soups

My mother was an excellent soup maker – she knew exactly how to get the correct ratio of stock to vegetables, meat and pulses so that the soup was hearty and nourishing without being heavy or stodgy. Growing up, soup was a weekend meal – there never seemed to be enough time for soup making during the week with both parents working. She always said 'the secret is in the stock'. And she was right.

Lamb and barley broth

This soup is comfort food and perfect for a cold winter's day, although my family will happily eat it all year round.

3 lean lamb shanks
2 litres water
2 onions, peeled and chopped
2 celery stalks with leaves, chopped
2 large carrots, chopped
1 potato, peeled and chopped
½ cup pearl barley
1 tablespoon rolled oats
parsley, finely chopped for serving
salt and pepper

Put the lamb shanks into the cold water and bring to the boil, simmering for 1½ hours, skimming off froth as it appears. Allow the broth to cool and refrigerate overnight so the fat rises to the surface and solidifies. Next day remove the fat and take out the shanks, chopping the meat from the bone and returning it to the stock. Add the chopped vegetables the barley, salt and pepper and simmer until the vegetables are cooked. Fifteen minutes before serving throw in the rolled oats – this slightly thickens the soup. Just before serving, add the finely chopped parsley.
cooking time 2½ hours • serves 4-6

Leek and potato soup

My mother often cooked this soup when we were young, and it was considered quite unusual in those days. This recipe comes from *The Flavour of France* and her old copy of the book is well splattered on page 54 where the soup, known as Potage Parisien, appears.

2 large leeks, cleaned and sliced very thinly
1 tablespoon butter
4 large potatoes, peeled and diced
5 cups boiling water
salt and pepper
4 tablespoons cream
small bunch of chives, finely chopped

Prepare the leeks and dry them with a paper towel, then sauté in the melted butter for about 5 minutes. Keep the flame low so that they soften but don't brown. Add the chopped potatoes and cook them gently in the butter, turning with a wooden spoon, for a further 5 minutes. Cover with the water and season with salt and pepper. Simmer gently for 30 minutes until the ingredients are soft. Use a masher to break up the potatoes and then a wire whisk to make the soup smooth. Add the cream at the last minute, taking care not to let it boil again. Garnish with the chopped chives and some extra pepper and a dab of butter.
cooking time 40 minutes • serves 4-6

Pea and ham soup

The addition of fresh mint at the end of the cooking process gives the soup a freshness that can otherwise be lacking. You can add extra water if you don't like pea soup too thick and, like most soups, it will taste better if cooked the day before.

500g green split peas
ham hock or leftover bone from a leg of ham
2.5 litres water
1 large potato, peeled and sliced
1 onion, peeled and diced
1 carrot, peeled and sliced
1 celery stalk with leaves, chopped
2 bay leaves
8 black peppercorns
sprig of mint
salt to taste

Wash and strain the split peas to remove impurities. Combine all the ingredients, except for the salt and the mint, in a large saucepan and bring to the boil. Lower the heat and skim the froth as it appears. The peas will take about 1½ hours to soften. The bone should then be lifted from the soup and the meat removed and chopped into small pieces. The rest of the soup should be allowed to cool a little then either sieved so that the vegetables can be mashed before being returned to the liquid or put through a food processor to make it smooth. I personally don't mind it being a bit chunky. Return the meat to the soup and add the spring of mint, allowing it to simmer for 5 minutes. Test for saltiness and add salt if required. Add more water if it's too thick for your taste and take care not to allow the peas to scorch on the bottom of the pan. Serve with sippets.
cooking time 1½ hours • serves 6-8

Sippets

These are crunchy and children, in particular, love adding them to soup after it's been served.

2 tablespoons olive oil
2 tablespoons butter
4-6 slices of stale bread, chopped into cubes

Heat the oil and butter in a heavy-based frying pan, taking care not to let it brown. Add the cubes of bread in small batches and turn carefully until both sides are brown and crispy. Add more butter and oil if it is absorbed by the bread. Serve immediately.
cooking time 5 minutes • serves 6-8

Mum's minestrone

I sometimes make vegetarian minestrone but it's never as tasty as this version, which relies on a really rich beef stock. Taking the trouble to make good stock makes all the difference to the end result.

2 thick pieces shin of beef
500g beef soup bones
2.5 litres cold water
2 tablespoons olive oil
2 onions, peeled and chopped
2 cloves of crushed garlic
2 leaves of silver beet, finely chopped
1 tomato, peeled and diced
2 celery stalks with leaves, chopped
2 large carrots, chopped
1 potato, peeled and chopped
300g tin kidney beans
12 sticks of spaghetti, broken into small lengths
1 tablespoon parsley, finely chopped

Make the stock the day before. Put the cold water into a soup pot then score the shin of beef deeply with a sharp knife to expose as much surface as possible. Put the beef and the bones into the water and allow them to stand for at least an hour so the blood leaches out of the meat into the water. Slowly bring to the boil and simmer for 1½ hours. The meat should be falling apart. Remove the meat and bones and refrigerate the stock overnight so that any fat rises to the surface and solidifies. The next day remove the fat and return the chopped meat to the stock. In a separate deep saucepan heat the olive oil and sauté the onion until translucent, then add the garlic and cook for a few minutes before tossing in the chopped silver beet, which should be allowed to wilt. Then add the tomato and let it soften – the flavours of these ingredients should be allowed to merge before the stock is poured over them. Add the chopped vegetables and kidney beans and simmer until the vegetables are well cooked. Fifteen minutes before serving throw in the spaghetti, then finally the parsley. Serve with grated Parmesan cheese and crusty bread.
cooking time 2 hours • serves 4-6

Chicken soup with dumplings

Dumplings are wonderful if they are light and fluffy and disappointing if stodgy and heavy. The secret is to have a light touch.

1 free range chicken (skin removed)
2.5 litres water
2 onions, peeled and chopped
2 celery stalks with leaves, chopped
2 large carrots, chopped
2 potatoes, peeled and chopped
½ green capsicum, chopped
1 tomato, peeled and deseeded then chopped
¼ cup rice
parsley, finely chopped
salt and pepper
dumplings
1¼ cups self-raising flour
½ teaspoon baking powder
75g cold butter, chopped
1 tablespoon very finely chopped parsley
pinch of salt
¼ cup cold water

Make the stock the day before. Put prepared chicken into the water and bring to the boil, then simmer for 1½ hours – slightly less if it's a smaller bird. Allow the stock to cool and refrigerate overnight so the fat rises to the surface and solidifies. Next day remove the fat and lift out the chicken, removing the flesh from the bones and tearing it by hand into small pieces. Keep this to one side – it should only be put back at the last minute. Add the chopped vegetables to the stock and cook for another hour at least, adding the rice 15 minutes before the end. Ten minutes before serving return the chicken meat to the soup, together with finely chopped parsley. Season to taste.
For the dumplings, sift the flour and baking powder together. Rub the butter into the flour by hand so it resembles fine breadcrumbs. Add the parsley. Make a well in the centre of the bowl and add the cold water, using a knife to mix it together into a sticky dough. Each dumpling should be about a tablespoon of dough, rolled roughly into a ball and dropped into the simmering soup. Put the lid on and cook for 10 minutes. The faster the whole procedure, the lighter the dumplings.
cooking time 2-3 hours • serves 6-8

Mum's minestrone

The Perfect Sunday Roast

Roasted meat with vegetables and gravy is probably the easiest family meal of all, but some people find it daunting. It's all in the timing. The aim is to get the meat just right – never overcooked; the potatoes and other roasted vegetables crispy; then the boiled or steamed vegetables cooked but never soggy! And then there's the gravy. I regard it as a bit of a juggling act but practice helps. I keep an eye on the clock and time the basic steps backwards from when I plan to serve the meal. Usually one o'clock for a Sunday lunch.

The timing

• The gravy is the last step, and it should take about 8-10 minutes.

• The steamed vegetables should take no longer than 12-15 minutes depending on what they are (carrots, beans, peas, spinach etc.) I use the water from the vegetables to make the gravy so they need to be cooked before the gravy is made and then kept hot in a double boiler or colander over a saucepan of simmering water.

• The meat can be taken out of the oven 20 minutes before carving and serving. It should be allowed to rest, which sets it and makes it easier to carve. But it should also be kept hot – I cover it with foil then put a clean tea towel over it to hold in some of the heat. If you have a warming oven the meat can be allowed to rest there.

• While the meat is resting I transfer the roasted vegetables (potatoes, pumpkin, parsnips, swedes etc) to a clean baking tray and put them on the top shelf of the oven – I often turn the oven up a bit and this really helps get the final crisp on them. Roasted vegetables take about an hour, depending on the size they have been cut.

• The meat should go into a moderate to hot (220°) oven into a roasting pan with about 3-4 tablespoons of hot oil or fat (I use a lot of goose fat for roasting). Plunging the meat into the hot oil seals the outside and helps prevent it from leaching blood. Turn it over after 5 minutes, and then turn the oven down to a medium heat (190°) because roasting at a high temperature dries out the meat and makes it tough.

Making the gravy

I make gravy in the pan in which I have roasted the meat using the juices and oil or fat – I always strain off the excess and only use about 2 tablespoons of fat as the basis. The pan should have little bits of meat and vegetables left from the roasting, and these add to the flavour and texture of the sauce. I then sprinkle on about 1 tablespoon of gravy flour (semolina – not to be confused with gravy maker) and have the pan on a hot plate (medium heat). Don't stir the flour into the fat immediately – let it brown but take care not to let it burn. Then mix with the fat and cook a bit more to take away any floury taste. The water reserved from boiling the vegetables is then added slowly, mixing all the time to prevent any lumpiness. You can also add a few tablespoons of red wine (especially if cooking roast beef) and any juices that have flowed from the meat while it was resting. I also save the fat and meat juices from previous roasts – storing them in the fridge and skimming the fat. This leaves a rich jelly that has an intense flavour. Some cooks recommend using stock for gravy – again to intensify the flavour – but I have always found that the little crispy bits of vegetable stuck to the pan, along with the water from the vegetables and meat juices, is quite sufficient.

Roast beef

My favourite cut is a wing rib, but an old fashioned rolled roast is an excellent alternative. For a dinner party you can also roast a scotch fillet or eye fillet because they are easy to carve. I rub a little salt and pepper into the meat and sometimes dust with a little flour because this helps to create extra crispy bits in the pan for making the gravy. Put the roasting pan in a moderate to hot (220°) oven with the oil or fat (or you can use a mixture of both) for 5 or 6 minutes then plunge the meat in, sealing one side. After 10 minutes turn it over to seal the other side then turn the oven down to 190° and cook for 30 minutes per kilo for a rare roast (the scotch fillet and eye fillet take less time than a wing rib on the bone). If cooking roasted potatoes, parboil them first so there will be time for them to cook for a while with the meat (before the meat is lifted).

Yorkshire pudding

My father's trick with Yorkshire pudding was to make the batter at least an hour before the cooking time (to allow the raising agent to work – it should have little bubbles on the surface before going into the oven). Preheat the ovenproof dish and pour in some of the meat juices and fat before adding the batter.

¾ cup self raising flour
pinch of salt
1 egg, lightly whisked
1 cup milk

Sift the flour and salt together then add the whisked egg and gradually stir in the milk, using a wire whisk to avoid lumps. Allow this to stand for at least an hour, adding a little extra milk if the batter seems too thick (it should be smooth and able to be poured, but not runny). Put an ovenproof dish in the oven, pouring some of the juices from the pan into the base. After this is hot (10 minutes) take the dish out of the oven and pour in the pudding batter. Cook for another 35-40 minutes, testing with a skewer in the middle to make sure it's done (if it's not done, some batter will stick to the skewer). You can also spoon some of the meat juices from the pan onto the top of the pudding as it rises – they will be absorbed and give the pudding an extra delicious flavour. If the oven is big enough you can alternatively cook a tray of individual puddings – either in muffin tins or small ramekins. These will cook much faster – maybe 15-20 minutes.
cooking time 40 minutes • serves 4-6

Retro recipes

Roast lamb and mint sauce

Roast lamb and mint sauce

A leg of lamb was always the most popular but these days the 'easy-carve' legs that have been boned work very well. I also love a shoulder of lamb, and again the supermarkets now sell them boned and rolled – the meat is sweeter than a leg but also a bit fattier.

Lamb goes well with garlic, with mint and with rosemary. The garlic can be inserted into the meat by using a sharp knife to puncture a hole, then pushing either a whole or half clove into it. A sprig of rosemary can be laid in the roasting pan, under the roast or chopped finely and sprinkled as a crust on the top. I sometimes crush chopped rosemary and sea salt in the mortar and pestle, and spread it thickly on the top of the lamb before putting it in the oven. Mint is usually made into a sauce or jelly and served at the table. While garlic and rosemary can be used together, mint is best served without any other herb.

The trick with lamb is to cook it slowly at a lower temperature than other meats – say about 170° – so that it remains juicy and moist. It dries out very quickly if cooked at a high temperature. I would cook a large leg of lamb for no more than 1½ hours – sometimes even less. And always allow it to stand, covered, for 20 minutes to set the juices. I baste the leg every 15-20 minutes with the juices from the pan. Roasted potatoes and pumpkin are particularly well flavoured when cooked in the same pan, and can be made crisp at the end, after the leg of lamb is lifted, by turning the temperature up (200°–220°) and moving the pan to the top of the oven.

mint sauce
⅓ cup sugar
½ cup boiling water
large sprig of mint, chopped finely
1 cup white vinegar

Dissolve the sugar in the boiling water, then add the chopped mint leaves and crush slightly with a fork to help the water take up some of the flavour. Add the vinegar and allow to rest for at least 30 minutes before serving.
preparation time 10 minutes • serves 6-8

Sausages in onion gravy

This was an alternative Friday night dish if it was too cold to go to the beach. Butcher-made sausages were very good in those days, although probably a little fattier than the good sausages available today. I use pork sausages that exude virtually no fat in the cooking. It's classic 'comfort' food.

1.5kg good quality sausages
oil for frying
1 tablespoon unsalted butter
4 onions, thinly sliced
2 tablespoons gravy flour
water
finely chopped parsley for parsley
salt and pepper

Prick the sausages. Heat enough oil in a heavy based frying pan to cover the base. Put in the sausages and cook for 20 minutes, turning until all sides are completely brown. Remove and keep warm. Add butter to the pan, then the sliced onions. Keep the pan on low and cook the onions until well softened and golden – never allow them to burn at the edges. You can cook the onions until they start to caramelise – up to 30 minutes. Lift the onions and tip out any excess oil – leaving about 1 tablespoon only. Add the flour and combine, cooking for a few minutes to remove the floury taste and to slightly brown the flour. Gradually stir in enough water to make a thick, brown gravy (add a little dark soy sauce if the gravy is pale). Return the onions and sausages to the gravy and heat through for 5-10 minutes. Sprinkle with finely chopped parsley and serve with mashed potatoes and peas or salad.
cooking time 45 minutes • serves 4-6

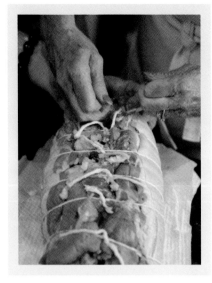

Roast pork and applesauce

My family prefers a leg of pork because there is more crackling and therefore less family squabbling. However a rolled loin is also delicious (see photograph opposite) – and for those who don't want to eat fatty crackling, there are also skinned rolled shoulders of pork that are less fattening. Like beef, pork needs to be started in a hot oven (220°) and then turned down to moderate (190°) for the cooking. I use fat (or vegetable oil) rather than olive oil because it reaches a higher temperature and helps to make the pork skin 'crackle'.

Use about 3 tablespoons of fat or oil and put your baking dish into a hot oven for 10 minutes until it's nice and hot (avoid letting it smoke). The butcher should have scored the pork fat with a sharp knife and it should be rubbed with about a tablespoon of salt – rub it well into the cracks. The leg is then plunged, skin side down, into the hot fat and returned to the oven for 15-20 minutes , then turned over and allowed to continue roasting at the high temperature for another 10 minutes before you turn the oven down to 190° for the rest of the cooking. The skin should continue to become crisp and bubbly. I cook a medium size leg of pork for 2 hours and rest it for 20 minutes before carving. The crackling can be removed in a sheet and put back into the oven to stay hot and crisp while the roasted potatoes and other vegetables are browning. If it fails to 'crackle' it can be rescued by being put under a hot grill for 5-10 minutes but it must be watched carefully as it can easily burn.
cooking time 2 hours • serves 6-8

Applesauce

3 Granny Smith apples, peeled and sliced
4 tablespoons water
1 tablespoon sugar

Put the apples, water and sugar into a small saucepan and cook until the apples are soft. Mash with a fork and allow to cool before serving.
cooking time 15-20 minutes • serves 6-8

Wiener Schnitzel

This version of a traditional Austrian recipe was brought back from America by my parents and was popular with the family because veal steaks were a bit of a treat in the Fifties and Sixties. A lot of traditional recipes call for the meat to be coated in breadcrumbs but my mother always used flour and added hot paprika for flavouring.

1 egg
2 tablespoons milk
salt and pepper
hot paprika
1 tablespoon plain flour
6 thin veal steaks, hammered flat with a meat mallet
oil for frying

Mix the egg and milk together. Add the salt and pepper and a good sprinkling of paprika to the flour. Dip the veal into the egg mixture then coat in the flour. Drop the veal immediately into a hot frying pan with oil covering the entire base. Cook on medium heat, turning once, for 12-15 minutes. Serve with lemon slices, hash brown potatoes (see page 44) and salad.
cooking time 20 minutes • serves 6

Mum's heavy cast-iron frying pans from America are still in constant use and I have no doubt my grandchildren will be using them one day.

Street photographs were all the rage in the Fifties and I have many of my parents, arm in arm, both in Sydney and New York.

Roast loin of pork

Weeknight meals

The life of a working mother in the 1950s wasn't easy, and as children we were expected to do chores to help keep the household running smoothly. There was no 'take-away' option and Mum somehow managed to put a balanced meal on the table every night in spite of her hectic schedule.

Corned beef, cabbage and white onion sauce

My grandsons from Adelaide adore this meal, even though it is so old-fashioned and most children loathe cabbage. When they come to stay and I ask what 'special meals' they would like me to make for them, corned beef and cabbage is usually their first choice.

2kg piece of corned beef
bay leaf
1 tablespoon brown sugar
black peppercorns
8-10 medium potatoes, peeled and washed
5 medium size carrots, peeled and sliced
half a head of cabbage, sliced finely
butter
salt and pepper
white onion sauce
1-2 white onions, diced
1 tablespoon butter
1 tablespoon flour
1¼ cups milk
salt and pepper

In a large, deep-sided saucepan cover the meat with cold water, adding the bay leaf, sugar and peppercorns. Bring to the boil then simmer for 1½ hours, until the meat is tender. You may need to skim the surface if scum appears. Twenty minutes before the meat is cooked the potatoes can be added. Lift the meat and set it to rest for 15 minutes. In the same water as the potatoes add the carrots and cook for 10 minutes. Lastly add the cabbage and cook for 5 minutes or slightly more – we like it well cooked but never soggy. Drain the vegetables and serve with the sliced corned beef, topped with hot white onion sauce. The vegetables should be dabbed with butter and seasoned to taste.

For the white sauce, boil the onions in a small saucepan, half filled with water. When translucent and tender (but not mushy) drain and reserve the liquid. Melt the butter in the saucepan, and then stir in the flour until combined. Cook a little bit, stirring so it doesn't burn. This helps to prevent a floury taste. Add the milk slowly, stirring with a wooden spoon, to make a smooth, lump-free sauce. It should be creamy. Return the onions to the sauce and cook for a few more minutes, thinning with some of the reserved water from boiling the onions, if the sauce gets thick. Season with salt and pepper and serve immediately.

cooking time 1½ - 2 hours (corned beef) •
cooking time 30 minutes (white sauce) • *serves 6-8*

Corned beef fritters

We love the day after a meal of corned beef because it means corned beef fritters. It's not the most slimming meal in the world, but certainly tasty and a great way of using up leftovers.

1½ cups plain flour
pinch of salt
2 eggs, whisked
1 cup milk, approximately
cooked corned beef
1 tablespoon butter
1 tablespoon olive oil

Sift the flour and salt into a mixing bowl. Add the eggs and then start mixing in the milk. The idea is to make a smooth batter, about the consistency of pancake batter. I use a wire whisk. Leave the batter to sit for 15 minutes.

Slice the cold corned beef. In a heavy-based frying pan heat the butter and olive oil. Dip the meat into the batter then fry – about 3-4 minutes each side – until crispy and heated through. Serve with tomato sauce and bubble and squeak if there are leftover vegetables. Go for a brisk walk afterwards to negate feelings of guilty pleasure.

cooking time 20 minutes

Old-fashioned
but adored
by all.

Corned beef, cabbage
and white onion sauce

Home-made pastry with a rich, meaty filling.

Steak and kidney pie

I vary this recipe according to family tastes – some of them like LOTS of kidney and some prefer just a suggestion. The kidney is what brings the flavour to the pie, but the texture of the meat is not universally enjoyed. I try to make the meat filling the day before to set the flavours – it needs to be cold before being put into the pastry so it should be made several hours in advance. You can also vary the recipe by adding a few cloves of finely chopped garlic or a tablespoon of tomato paste. Or both.

We often spent a few hours at the beach before the Sunday lunch, working up a good appetite.

1kg shin of beef, cut into cubes
500g lamb kidney, trimmed and finely sliced
1 tablespoon plain flour
salt and pepper
1-2 tablespoons olive oil
1 onion, peeled and chopped
1-2 cups of water
splash of red wine
shortcrust pastry
1½ cups plain flour, sifted
salt
¾ cup cold, unsalted butter, chopped
small quantity cold water
1 tablespoon milk

Put the diced meats into a plastic bag with the flour, salt and pepper and shake until lightly coated. Heat the oil in a heavy-based saucepan and cook the onion until soft and translucent. Set the onion aside, add some more oil to the pan and brown the meat in small batches. Return all the meat and the onion to the pan and add the water and wine. Turn down the temperature to the lowest possible simmer and cover the pan. Cook for 1½ hours, stirring regularly to prevent the meat from sticking to the base of the pan. This meat with its thick, rich gravy should be set aside to cool.

To make the pastry, first sift the flour and salt and put into a food processor with the finely chopped, cold butter. Process until the mix looks like fine breadcrumbs. I like the water REALLY cold and add a tablespoon at a time until it forms a solid dough. Be light handed with the food processor as the less handling, the better the pastry. Wrap with cling wrap and put into the fridge for 30 minutes. Roll half the pastry on a well-floured board (or cool marble slab) and line a well-buttered pie dish. Fill with the cold meat mixture and use a pastry brush to apply water around the edge so that the two layers of pastry will stick together well. I also put a pie bird in the middle to lift the pastry in the centre and act as a steam vent. Roll out the pastry for the pie top, cutting a small X in the centre to slip over the head of the pie bird. Trim away any excess pastry and use a fork, dipped in flour to press the pastry edges together. If you aren't using a pie bird simply cut a couple of slits in the pastry top to allow the steam to escape. Glaze the top with the milk and cook in a hot (200º) oven until the pastry is brown – 35-45 minutes. Serve with baked or mashed potatoes and a green vegetable or salad.
cooking time 2-3 hours • serves 4-6
• Frozen pastry can be used as a quick alternative – some people prefer their pie with flaky pastry, which can also be bought, pre-rolled and frozen.

Retro recipes

Vegetables

The basic vegetables of the era reflected traditional English cuisine. We always had a selection of at least four different vegetables at each meal and the leftovers were used the following morning to make bubble and squeak.

Hash brown potatoes

My parents brought the concept of potato 'hash' back from America after the War, and as a child it was my favourite way of eating potatoes. We eat them with eggs for breakfast, or with steak or grilled lamb chops at dinnertime.

1.5kg mashing potatoes, peeled and washed
2 tablespoons olive oil
1 tablespoon butter
salt

Chop the potatoes into quarters and parboil in salted water until half cooked (12-15 minutes). Drain and allow the potatoes to dry thoroughly. Heat the oil and butter in a heavy based frying pan. Roughly chop the parboiled potatoes – the idea is to have different sized pieces. Put all the potatoes into the pan of hot oil. The trick is not to be tempted to turn them too often – they need to really get crispy before being turned – the temperature should remain quite high and this heat will finish cooking the potatoes while crisping them at the same time. If the potatoes completely absorb the oil add a little more. Lift onto a paper towel and sprinkle with salt before serving.
cooking time 15 minutes • serves 4-6

Cauliflower cheese

This is another side dish to serve with a roast. It is also good with chops or steak and leftovers. Can be reheated and served on toast for breakfast or thrown into a mix of bubble and squeak.

1 small to medium head of cauliflower, leaves removed
water to cover
cheese sauce
2 tablespoons butter
2 tablespoons flour
milk
1½ cups grated cheddar cheese (or half and half with Parmesan)
salt and pepper
pinch cayenne pepper

If the head of cauliflower is small I sometimes cook and serve it whole, while a larger one is broken into small florets. Cook cauliflower in salted water until a skewer can pass through easily – but never allow to overcook and go soft. Drain and put into a deep-sided ovenproof dish.
Melt the butter in the pan in which the cauliflower was cooked. Mix in the flour and allow to cook for several minutes to remove the floury taste. Gradually add the milk and stir with a wire whisk to prevent lump. Adding the milk too quickly will definitely cause lumps! The amount of milk will depend on the consistency you prefer – I like it quite runny because it continues to thicken as it cooks in the oven. Add the cheese, salt, pepper and cayenne and pour over the cauliflower. If you like, sprinkle a little extra grated cheese on top and put in the oven for 15-20 minutes. It should be bubbling and lightly brown on top.
cooking time 40 minutes • serves 4-6

Bubble & squeak

This was one of my favourite breakfasts as a child, usually served the morning after a meal of corned beef and cabbage. Cooked leftover vegetables are fried in oil until they're crisp. Season and serve with a fried egg or grilled lamb chop and buttered toast.

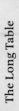

Cauliflower cheese

Desserts

We usually only had homemade desserts at the weekends – particularly for Sunday lunch – because there wasn't enough time during the week. Mum was a great believer in the fruit bowl as an alternative.

Apple snow

This is the lightest and freshest of desserts and is quick to make and generally loved by children. We eat it on its own – in a tall glass like a parfait.

6-8 large Granny Smith apples, peeled and sliced
1 cup of sugar
2 egg whites
2 passionfruit

Cook the apples and sugar in a small amount of water – just enough to stop them from sticking until their own juices are extracted by the heat. They should not be too watery when cooked – if so, strain off some of the excess liquid. Allow to cool slightly. Whisk the egg whites until they form firm peaks. Add the passionfruit pulp to the apples then fold the egg whites into the apple mixture – keeping it as light as possible until well combined. Serve chilled.
cooking time 20-30 minutes • serves 4-6

Baked apples

This is David's favourite dessert.
He would have it every night except
he now has to watch his sugar intake.

6 large Granny Smith apples, cored but not peeled
enough dried dates to fill the apples
1 tablespoon brown sugar per apple
3 cloves per apple
½ teaspoon butter per apple

Wipe the outside of the cored apples and place them
in a shallow, buttered ovenproof dish. Pack some dates
into the hole in the centre, then some brown sugar,
some more dates and so on until the apples are stuffed
to overflowing. Prick several holes in the apple skin
with a skewer to allow the steam to escape and also
insert a few cloves to add flavour. Top each with a dab
of butter and cook in a moderate (190°) oven for
20 minutes, checking with a skewer to see if the
apples are cooked – they need to be hot and fluffy but
not overcooked because they will split and collapse.
Serve with cream or pouring custard.
cooking time 30 minutes • serves 6

Baked egg custard

I make this at least once a week and can
do it blindfolded. It's great when you have
plenty of free-range eggs and I always
use less sugar than most recipes so it's
actually quite a healthy dessert, served
with stewed rhubarb.

600ml full cream milk
1 cup raw sugar
3 drops vanilla essence
4 large eggs
sprinkle of nutmeg

Heat the milk in a saucepan with the sugar and vanilla,
stirring with a wooden spoon until the sugar dissolves.
The milk should just about reach scalding point.
In a separate bowl beat the eggs, they should be
thoroughly combined but not too fluffy. Add the hot
milk, whisking all the time to make sure the whites
don't get stringy. Lightly butter a shallow ovenproof
dish and place in a baking dish of water (coming
halfway up the sides of the custard dish). This means
the custard is poached instead of baked. Use a fine
sieve and strain the custard mixture into this dish
– this removes any stringy bits of egg or fluff. Sprinkle
lightly with nutmeg and place in a moderate oven
(185°) and cook for 25 minutes – test with a skewer
into the centre of the custard – if it comes out clean
the custard is cooked. If egg still adheres, cook for a
further 5-10 minutes. Lift the custard dish from the
poaching pan and allow to cool to room temperature
before serving.
cooking time 30-40 minutes • serves 4-6

The family in America
during the War: Margaret,
Mum, Jon and Dad.

Banana custard

Banana custard

This is such an Australian twist to pouring custard, and as children we absolutely loved it. Sometimes my mother would cheat and use custard powder, but generally she would make 'real' custard using the double boiler she brought back from America.

2 cups full cream milk
2 eggs plus 2 egg yolks
2 tablespoons sugar
3 bananas, peeled and sliced

In the top of a double boiler heat the milk until warm but not scalding. If you don't have a double boiler use a heatproof bowl over a saucepan of water – in both cases the water should be boiling underneath but not actually touching the base of the bowl. Whisk the eggs and sugar together and mix this into the milk, continuing to heat and stir with a wooden spoon until the custard starts to thicken. The water underneath should be at a low simmer – if it is boiling too vigorously the custard will curdle. In fact the custard should never boil – just be on the edge so that it thickens to a smooth, creamy consistency. As soon as it reaches this point take the custard off the heat and add the sliced bananas. It should be eaten the same day because the bananas will turn brown overnight.
cooking time 15-25 minutes • serves 4

Queen of puddings

This is a basic baked egg custard with an extra treat on top – some jam and lightly cooked meringue. It's a favourite with the grandchildren and they always polish off every last skerrick – picking the crusty meringue bits from the sides of the baking bowl.

600ml full cream milk
1 cup raw sugar
½ cup caster sugar (1 egg) or ¾ cup (2 eggs)
3 drops vanilla essence
4 large eggs
1 or 2 extra eggs separated (depending on how
    much meringue you want)
2 tablespoons plum or berry jam

Heat the milk in a saucepan with the sugar and vanilla, stirring with a wooden spoon until the sugar dissolves. The milk should just about reach scalding point. Separate one or two eggs, setting aside the whites. In a separate bowl beat the other 4 eggs and the yolk from the separated egg, making sure they are thoroughly combined but not too fluffy. The extra yolk will just make the custard richer. Add the hot milk, whisking all the time to make sure the whites don't get stringy. Lightly butter a shallow ovenproof dish and place in a baking dish of water (coming halfway up the sides of the custard dish). This means the custard is poached instead of baked. Use a fine sieve and strain the custard mixture into this dish – this removes any stringy bits of egg or fluff. Place in a moderate oven (185°) and cook for 25 minutes – test with a skewer into the centre of the custard – if it comes out clean the custard is cooked. If egg still adheres, cook for a further 5-10 minutes. While the custard cooks whisk the egg whites until they form peaks then gradually add the sugar until completely dissolved. Remove the custard from the oven, still in the poaching dish, and smother the top of the hot custard with the jam – it will melt as you spread it. Spoon the meringue onto the top, making a nice covering with peaks. Turn oven up to 200° and put the custard back in for another 5-10 minutes until the peaks have browned. Cool slightly before serving.
cooking time 40 minutes • serves 4-6

It was the busiest and happiest time of my life.

Raising

he family

I left home at eighteen

and joined *The Australian Women's Weekly* magazine as a cadet (trainee) journalist, following in the footsteps of my parents. I lived in a group house in trendy Paddington and the five friends I shared with were either students or unemployed. I was the only one with a paying job ($29.75 a week) and even though my flatmates threw money into the food kitty, I was the one who ended up doing most of the shopping and cooking on a very tight budget.

We were saved by the magazine's test kitchen. Every afternoon I would go down to the studio where the recipes were being tried out and see what was on offer. For 15-20 cents I could pick up a large container of beef stew or casserole, a tuna and rice dish or even a pie or quiche (quite an avant garde recipe in those days). Sometimes the food was pretty ghastly – failed recipes that would never appear on the magazine pages. But we ate it anyway, grateful for cheap food that had been prepared by somebody else!

One evening I was invited to a dinner party at the home of a work colleague. She served spaghetti bolognaise which I had never even heard of, let alone eaten – beef mince in our house was used only to make meatloaf, savoury mince or shepherd's pie. Spaghetti without the toast – how quaint! My friend must have done her research properly because she served the pasta and rich sauce with a side salad, crusty bread and grated Parmesan cheese. I took one sniff of the cheese and recoiled – it was revolting. The cheese we ate in those days was a simple, rather bland cheddar and it took years before my palate adjusted to the more exotic and flavoursome cheeses imported from the northern hemisphere.

Even when I first left home, I enjoyed cooking for people.

As a young woman I loved working on magazines; the training we were given was 'hands on' rather than academic. It was a matter of sink or swim.

In the sixties and seventies fashionable food was fiddly; somehow I was always drawn back to the simple favourites.

I started collecting 'kitsch' retro cookbooks and these days I marvel at how truly frightful many of the recipes were – I can't believe we actually cooked and ate them.

In the late 1960s and early 1970s the popular cuisine was kitsch. While the inspiring works of the English food writer Elizabeth David had filtered through to the more sophisticated and well travelled 'foodies' with cookbooks written by the likes of Graham Kerr and Robert Carrier, the rest of the population followed recipes in best-selling cookbooks that were advocating lashings of tinned pineapple and sliced beetroot. To say the food was colourful is an understatement. In recent years I have scoured second-hand shops in search of some of the cookbooks from that unfortunate era and I have accumulated an impressive and hilarious collection including *The Golden Circle Tropical Recipe Book*, *Modern Gelatine Cookery* and Margaret Fulton's *100 Hostess Party Favourites*. The recipes and photographs are outrageous, and among my favourite concoctions from the *Hostess* book are:

Ham and Banana Chip Rolls: this involves dipping halved bananas in lemon juice and rolling them in crushed potato chips then wrapping them in sliced ham and cooking them under a hot grill.

Spam Salad San Francisco: combines cold cooked rice with thin slices of tinned spam, chopped shallots and cooked frozen peas, sprinkled with parsley.

My early dinner parties as a single girl living away from home aimed to impress with elaborate recipes such as Beef Stroganoff, Chicken Cacciatore, Carpetbag Steak and Beef Wellington. Fondues were all the rage, with a candlelit centrepiece of bubbling cheese sauce and long skewers for the dipping of various meats and vegetables into the calorie-rich mix. My standard first course was a chicken liver pâté served with squares of toast, and then I usually made a cheesecake of some description for dessert. Compared to the three (or even five) course meals I serve today, these dinners were unbalanced and unhealthy because every dish was rich and fatty and there wasn't enough salad or vegetables. Just imagine. Cream in the pâté, cream in the stroganoff and cream IN and ON the cheesecake. I got better.

life was such an adventure and I embraced it totally...

I met David in 1971 when we were both working at Channel 9 – he as a television producer and me in publicity. We 'moved in' together and bought a semi-detached cottage with a small kitchen which I renovated with bright wallpaper and shelving. It was fairly hideous. I reverted to cooking my old favourite family recipes because they were more economical and authentic – not just fad or fashion. I also knew them off by heart and didn't have to constantly refer to a cookbook for methods and measurements. However I did have a copy of *Commonsense Cookery* from my high school home economics class and, when it was first published, I bought *The Australian Family Circle Cookbook* because it had a wide range of great ideas that suited our lifestyle and our budget.

When our children came along I enthusiastically introduced them to 'solid' food, probably long before it was really necessary, shovelling mashed brains and sieved vegetables into their toothless little mouths from the age of twelve weeks. When I compare this to how my grandchildren are being reared on a diet of nothing but breast milk for at least six months, I realise that it must have been a reflection of my nurturing disposition. I am driven to feed people, regardless of common sense. Fortunately my force-feeding didn't have any long-term repercussions and the children developed an interest in what they were eating from a very early age. Our daughter Miriam's first structured sentence was 'what's for dinner, Mum?' Very telling.

During the period when the children were toddlers I became interested in the health implications of chemicals in the food chain. I read a lot about the vast quantities of chemical fertilisers, insecticides and herbicides used in commercial food production and this reading convinced me that I should be feeding my growing family only with organically-grown produce. The article that polarised my views described the use of Valium in battery egg production. Back in those days some hens housed in large tin sheds were fed a layer mash that contained tranquillisers to keep them docile during mid-summer when heatwave conditions prevailed. I was so horrified I immediately stopped buying eggs and introduced a couple of friendly bantams to the backyard. However, two tiny eggs a day wasn't enough to supply a family of our size and appetite.

David was now working in the film industry, which was based in Sydney. I decided that for lifestyle reasons the entire family should move to a rural area where I could grow

125

Setting up house with David was fun and having babies was the most joyful experience of my life. Here on the front verandah of our Sydney cottage with Miriam at six days old. (Why am I holding her like a sack of potatoes?)

I decorated my first kitchen with gaudy Seventies wallpaper and lots of brown and orange gadgets. At the time I thought it just perfect.

Miriam, Aaron, Tony and Ethan in fancy dress leaving for the school fete.

our own organic vegetables, herbs and fruit – ideally becoming semi-self-sufficient. It was a typical dream of the Seventies (remember the *Good Life* television series?) I didn't know anything about gardening, having spent my entire childhood living in a block of flats, but that didn't discourage me. Our weekends were spent driving to the Blue Mountains in search of a property. While I still yearned for acreage and a 'proper farm', David wisely suggested we compromise and live no more than two hours from the city.

My father died just before our first child was born, and then around the time we were looking to move out of Sydney my mother came to live in our little two-bedroom cottage. She had injured her leg and needed nursing to get back on her feet. With three adults and two small children living under the one small roof, the need to move to a larger house became even more urgent. After months of searching we found a wonderful four-bedroom weatherboard house at Leura with a large enough garden for me to realise my dream of running a mini-farm.

The first three things I did were to rip out the modern gas heater (much to David's horror) and reinstate the traditional open fireplace in the living room; to pull out a cupboard in the kitchen fireplace and install a second-hand wood-burning cooker that would also heat our domestic water for washing and showers (it was a Rayburn); and to rotary-hoe half the backyard to establish a large and comprehensive vegetable garden.

In opening up the fireplaces I created a tremendous amount of work for myself, chopping and stacking wood and keeping the cooking stove alight all year round. However this was never a problem – I was young, passionate and energetic and I believed I was

Raising the family

The soil was dry and sandy but
within a few years I had enriched it
with so much compost and manure that
I could pack a tremendous amount of
produce into a compact space. It was
deeply satisfying.

I experimented with growing as
many different vegetables,
herbs and fruits as possible
in the cool climate.

The children came home to a warm kitchen and welcoming grandma.

Fresh scones were a favourite,
often served with jams or jellies
that I made on the woodstove
using fruit from the garden.
It was more fun than hard work.

My mother adored her grandchildren and because she lived with us I was able to continue working as a freelance writer. Her contribution to the family was invaluable.

doing exactly the right thing for my expanding family. I devoured gardening magazines and books and did surprisingly well – within six months of moving in we were enjoying our first harvest of summer vegetables.

I built a rough chook house with old bricks and rehabilitated three middle-aged battery hens that were due to be executed.

'They'll never lay for you, they are too old,' the cynical farmer advised me. But within a month I was getting three brown eggs a day and one of the hens chose to lay her eggs in the wood basket next to the fuel stove.

Of necessity David had to live in Sydney from Monday to Friday to work, so we established a routine of hard working weeks and relaxing family weekends. The Sunday roast was back on the menu! Ironically my enthusiasm for gardening evolved into a career as I was approached by publishers to use my journalistic skills to write magazine articles and to edit gardening books. I didn't write in the tone of an 'expert' but as a passionate amateur, and this meant I could work from home while the children were at school and still find time to garden and cook. A perfect life.

By this time my mother had fully recovered and she loved living in the mountains and delighted in helping me care for the children and tend the large, somewhat unruly garden. We were a team and we had so much fun watching the fruit trees grow, gathering the eggs and picking fresh vegetables in the afternoon for the evening meal. I bought a Fowlers' bottling kit and started making my own fruit and vegetable preserves, as well as hams and pickles and chutneys, using as much of our own produce as possible.

Mum often walked the children to school and then walked back in the afternoon to get them. She also made them afternoon tea – every afternoon. Scones or pikelets or biscuits or French toast – seldom cake, as neither of us were great cake-bakers. Unlike my

Family times together were the
happiest and we loved the hot, dry
summers and snowy winters of Leura.

own childhood, where I came home to an empty flat every afternoon, our children came
home to a warm kitchen, a welcoming Grandma and something delicious to eat.

There was usually soup on the wood stove in winter and the children would
change out of their school uniforms before having some soup followed by something
sweet made by Grandma. When they had finished their afternoon tea – I took a tough
line on snacking – they could play outside, or watch one hour of television or do their
homework but they would not be allowed to eat anything – apart from a piece of fruit
– between afternoon tea and dinnertime. I loved the way they would come in and sniff the
air, taking in the aromas of the meal in the oven and ask to have a look. When Miriam was
about six she asked to see the rabbit stew I was slow cooking – she peered thoughtfully
into the pot and asked 'where are the ears?' The concept of a little fluffy bunny being
eaten had no effect on her – food was food and they were a hungry tribe.

Of course they drove me mad, pestering me for something to eat in that
exasperating hour before we sat down to the table, but I was adamant. There's nothing
wrong with children being hungry (or anyone for that matter) for a little while because it
gets the taste buds and gastric juices going and encourages them to eat their meal and not
pick at it – as children do who have been snacking on salty or sugary treats all afternoon.
These days we live in a world of instant gratification where at the slightest hunger pang we
grab something to satisfy our appetite. I remember as a child feeling absolutely starving
when I sat down to eat and I believe it made me appreciate the food more (we also weren't
allowed to bolt it down, which of course is the natural tendency when feeling that hungry).

Cosy winters spent in front of an open fire

Miriam helping
with the harvest

The garden was ornamental
as well as productive; I
loved old-fashioned
flowers best of all.

The children grew up loving animals and gardens. Two of my sons went on to study horticulture.

The children often helped themselves to vegetables straight from the garden. I would find them eating tomatoes warm from the sun.

We kept chickens and ducks for eggs and manure. The ducks were also good for keeping snails and slugs under control.

The original Rayburn was old but cooked brilliantly. I baked bread all year round, allowing it to rise in an old pudding bowl on the hearth in front of the warm stove.

I was also quite stringent about packaged or processed foods – we simply didn't buy them. No take-aways, no frozen meals, no sweets or chocolates for that matter – children's birthday parties were healthy affairs with carrot and celery sticks and cheese squares followed by wholemeal sandwiches and mini pies. Anything sweet was homemade and we always halved the sugar content of the recipe and totally avoided all colourings, preservatives and flavourings. My adult children now tease me about my rigid 'healthy food' regime while they were growing up, especially as I am much more indulgent these days with my grandchildren!

My final sticking point was eating at the table – breakfast, lunch and dinner. No meals in front of the television – the only exception was on Sunday nights in winter when we would sometimes make jaffles over the open fire. I had an old jaffle iron belonging to my mother – I remember using it on the open fire in our flat as a child and this is no doubt where I developed my love of the comforting flickering flames. A jaffle iron is the old-fashioned equivalent of a toasted sandwich maker. The bread is buttered and placed in the iron, buttered side outwards. The filling is added – ham, cheese, tomato, anything – and the iron is snapped shut and held over the coals until the toasty aroma indicates it is cooked. We once used the jaffle iron almost every night for six weeks while our new kitchen (and the long table) were being built. For the first fortnight the children were thrilled with this informal dining, but the novelty soon wore off and they were delighted when we finally had the stove back and were able to enjoy a proper roast dinner.

For years I only cooked on the wood-burning Rayburn, becoming adept and getting the heat up quickly in the late afternoon and damping it down so it would keep going overnight. I leapt out of bed early, opened out the flue and put the kettle on for tea then started the porridge as the fire warmed. I loved having a fire going and it certainly

Our neighbours often came for lunch;
David's family including his mother
(Mary) visiting from New Zealand
and my extended family, of course.
Christmas, holidays and birthdays -
any excuse for a party!

A constant stream of family and friends.

kept the kitchen cosy in winter because Leura has a cold climate and none of the houses have central heating. Nothing bakes or roasts better than a wood stove, and for years I made wholemeal and rye bread, leaving it on the hearth to prove every morning. I also brewed our own beer in a plastic garbage bin that was positioned near the stove so the constant warmth could assist fermentation.

We slotted easily into the Blue Mountains' community, which had more than its fair share of city escapees as well as a large creative and artistic community. We met poets and scriptwriters, journalists, painters, designers, sculptors, musicians, actors, photographers, teachers and (of course) politicians and environmental activists. We developed a rich and diverse social life that began with our nearest neighbours and extended the length and breadth of the region.

One of our most memorable visitors was the Indian/English film producer Ishmael Merchant of Merchant Ivory fame. He and David were working on a film together and he stayed for two weeks in a nearby hotel. Ishmael was as famous a cook as he was a filmmaker, and after a few days he asked if he could use my kitchen to cook for our family and the visiting pre-production crew. I followed him around the local shops then watched him prepare meals while taking notes – his recipes were largely his own invention and were probably the most delicious curries I have eaten in my life. Several years later David bumped into him at the American film market and he sent me a copy of his latest cookbook, which I treasure to this day. Sadly Ishmael died suddenly a few years ago – I still cook his lemon lentils, which everyone loves.

We had endless dinner parties and weekend visitors from the city who loved to curl up in front of the open fire after lunch. Every Guy Fawkes' night we would light a massive bonfire and cook up two or three different soups and bake fresh bread, then make mulled wine to drink around the fire while the designated responsible adult set off the firecrackers.

For ten years I was a presenter on the ABC's *Gardening Australia* TV show and we routinely fed the film crews that visited once a month to film segments for the program. These evenings were always outrageous fun, and my mother in particular loved the stimulation of a television program being shot in our own backyard.

We had several large parties, involving marquees and catering for up to 100 people at a time. David's 45th birthday was a memorable one (we came dressed as a bride and groom because we hadn't, as yet, managed to get married). When we did marry (after 22 years) we had the legendary chef Michael Manners prepare a wonderful six-course lunch, which was enjoyed by our friends and family in the garden, under a marquee. It was fun to have our grown-up and teenage children joining our wedding festivities.

Family group in kitchen

Jenny Kee at our wedding

Aaron and Lorna's wedding

Tony and Simone's wedding

There were four weddings in the garden; David and I after 22 years together followed by Tony and Simone, Miriam and Richard and Aaron and Lorna. Every time we had perfect weather.

Television personality Noni Hazlehurst and well-known artist Jenny Kee were neighbours - it was an artistic and creative community and a great environment for raising children.

Noni Hazlehurst and our young family on the back verandah

Miriam and Rick getting married

David and I getting married

Mum with her first
great-grandchild –
Eamonn – at three months.
Our adult children and
their partners: Tony and
Simone, Rick and Miriam,
Lorna and Aaron, Lynne
and Ethan.

Eventually three of our children were also married in the garden. First Tony and Simone (1994); they opted for a spring garden ceremony followed by a wedding breakfast at spectacular restaurant overlooking the Jamison Valley; then Miriam and Rick who had a very small group of family and friends in the garden followed by lunch in the famous Silks restaurant in Leura; and finally Aaron and Lorna who wanted both the ceremony and the wedding breakfast at home. I put a lot of effort into the garden – planting 500 daffodils on the edge of the top lawn that were guaranteed to bloom on the week of the wedding (they did); and all the women in the family (my daughter and daughters-in-law) helped with the catering. It was a splendid day.

My mother Muriel died suddenly in 1997 and we had a home funeral where friends and family gathered in the kitchen, spilling out onto the verandah and garden. In the Irish tradition we held a vigil, with her coffin on the kitchen table for two days and nights. All our children and their friends painted and decorated the coffin and then the night before the funeral we had a party in her honour in the kitchen. I cooked a huge pot of Irish stew and we celebrated, as she would have so enjoyed, drinking Guinness and wine, and reminiscing about all the funny and happy times we had had together (and some of the sad times too).

On the morning of the funeral David spoke to the gathering in the garden. I call it his 'four weddings and a funeral' speech. Together we acknowledged the great joy we had shared in the Leura house and garden, the mayhem of our large extended family and the fact that it had been 'open house' for 25 years, with the warm kitchen and the long table at the heart of our lives.

The house felt empty when the children finally left.

I adored roses, especially old-fashioned varieties and David Austins.

As the children grew and left home the garden became an even more important facet of my life. I often spent the whole day outside, lost in the joys of working with the soil.

Breakfasts

Following in my mother's footsteps I usually made a cooked breakfast for the children before school. We had so many eggs available and because TV was banned in the morning there was time to sit around the table and talk.

Special scrambled eggs

We love plain scrambled eggs because the eggs that our chickens produce have such wonderful golden yolks. However it's fun to liven them up with some tasty extras.

1 tablespoon butter
1 onion, very finely chopped
I lean rasher of bacon, finely chopped
6-8 eggs
1 tablespoon milk
salt and pepper
1 tomato, peeled, seeded and chopped

Melt the butter in a heavy-based frying pan and gently sauté the onion until soft and translucent. Add the bacon and cook for several minutes. Whisk the eggs and milk and season with salt and pepper. Add this to the pan and gently scramble on a low heat, stirring to prevent the eggs from sticking. When the eggs are starting to set add the tomato and stir slightly less often (or the tomato will make it mushy). Take the pan from the heat before the eggs have finished cooking – they will keep cooking while you are serving them onto buttered toast (we don't like our scrambled eggs to go hard – they should still be a bit mushy).
cooking time 10-12 minutes • serves 4

Family recipes

Coddled eggs

These are very liked poached eggs, but cooked in a teacup (or special egg coddler) in a pan of simmering water. My mother cooked them for us as children when we were sick, and she did the same for my children when we all lived together.

eggs
butter
salt and pepper

Half fill a deep, flat-bottomed frying pan (one that has a lid) with water. Bring to the boil then turn down to simmer. Grease the inside of the teacups with butter and break in one or two eggs, seasoning with salt and pepper. Put the cups into the frying pan (the water should be two-thirds of the way up the sides of the cups) and put the lid on. Simmer for 7-8 minutes. Sprinkle a little finely chopped parsley on top or, if feeling adventurous, a dash of chilli sauce. Eat straight from the cup accompanied by brown bread and butter.
cooking time 7-8 minutes

Stewed tomatoes on toast

This is comfort food for the end of summer when the tomatoes from the garden are at their peak. Choose the reddest and ripest tomatoes and serve with thickly sliced brown bread toast, well-buttered.

1 tablespoon butter
1kg ripe tomatoes, peeled and quartered
½ teaspoon Tabasco sauce
salt and pepper

In a heavy-based frying pan heat the butter until melted then add the chopped and peeled tomatoes, turning the stove down to low. Cook slowly – they need to 'stew' rather than fry. Just before serving add the Tabasco or a teaspoon of very finely chopped parsley or chives, salt and pepper.
cooking time 20 minutes • serves 4

Country breakfast

Country breakfast

We only do this three or four times a year because it's high in fat and rather an indulgence. Late morning is a good time to serve this, skipping lunch and going for a long afternoon walk before dinner.

4 good pork sausages
olive oil for frying
4 medium tomatoes, halved
4 rashers of bacon, rind removed
4 parboiled potatoes, roughly chopped
4-6 eggs (some people like 2 eggs each)
chopped parsley for garnish
salt and pepper

You need about three good frying pans for this. The secret is to never have the heat too high, except for the potatoes, which need extra heat to finish cooking and for browning.

Prick the sausages and put them in one of the pans with about 1 tablespoon of olive oil. Cook slowly and when half cooked (about 12 minutes) put the tomatoes in the pan, cut side downwards. In the second pan start cooking the bacon in a little olive oil – it will produce bacon fat that can be used later for frying the eggs. In the third pan make hash brown potatoes (see page 44). After 4 minutes turn the tomatoes upside down. Keep turning the bacon and sausages until evenly brown. Lift the bacon and put it on top of the sausages to keep it warm while the eggs are frying. I always fry eggs on low heat – but some people prefer the edges of the whites to turn brown in which case the heat can be turned up a little. While the eggs are cooking get someone to make the toast and serve onto warmed plates, garnish with parsley and season with salt and pepper. A breakfast like this should be accompanied by freshly squeezed orange juice and extra toast should be served at the end with lashings of jam or honey.
cooking time 25-30 minutes • serves 4

Breakfast burgers

My grandchildren know that I have a loathing for fast food chains. So I cook them homemade burgers – either for breakfast or lunch – and they infinitely prefer them. If I make them for breakfast I add a fried egg and at lunchtime they like mustard and a slice of cheese and bacon. Unless you have several frying pans going at once, these will need to be cooked in batches of four.

beef patties
1 slice stale bread
¾ cup milk
1kg lean beef mince
1 egg
1 onion, finely diced
salt and pepper
extras
1 tablespoon olive oil
1 tablespoon butter
2 onions sliced thinly
8 eggs
8 good quality bread rolls
butter
2 tomatoes, sliced thinly
shredded lettuce
alfalfa sprouts
tomato sauce

In a mixing bowl soak the stale bread in the milk until soft. Add the other ingredients and mix thoroughly by hand. Form into meat patties that are the same size as the bread rolls and approx 3-4 cm thick.

Put the olive oil and butter in a heavy-based frying pan and heat until butter is melted but not smoking. Add the sliced onions and turn down the heat, cooking them slowly for 15 minutes until soft and partially caramelised. Lift and drain on a paper towel. Cook the beef patties in the same pan for about 8 minutes each side. Lift and keep warm. Now fry the eggs, on low heat, to prevent the whites from burning. Cut the bread rolls in half and toast the inside under the grill. Butter the rolls and then assemble the burgers – first the meat patty followed by onions, tomato, lettuce and alfalfa sprouts and tomato sauce.
cooking time 30 minutes • serves 8

Soups

Soup was our equivalent of fast food. During winter, in particular, there would always be a pot simmering on the hob and we added to it constantly by chopping up leftovers and using the water from boiling vegetables as stock. It was the ultimate in recycling!

Tomato and basil soup

This summer soup can be served hot or cold and has the most intense flavour. It is popular in France during summer when fresh basil grows in abundance. The best tomatoes for this are beefsteak (coeur de boeuf) which are the largest, fleshiest variety in cultivation.

1 tablespoon butter or good olive oil
1 onion, peeled and chopped
1.5kg tomatoes, peeled and seeded
½ cup basil leaves, chopped
4-6 cups chicken stock
salt and pepper

In a heavy-based soup pot melt the butter or heat the oil and sauté the onion until soft and translucent. Add the tomatoes and basil and stir for a few minutes so that the flavours combine. Cover with the stock and bring to the boil, then turn down to a low simmer and cook for 30 minutes or more. This soup is best if smooth, so put it through a food processor in batches. Serve with sippets (see page 31) or crusty white bread followed by cheese and a green salad.
cooking time 35 minutes • serves 4

Pumpkin soup

At the end of summer there are always butternut pumpkins on the vine, which make the sweetest soup. There are lots of things you can do to spice up this basic recipe – add cumin and turmeric or some chilli. But with home-grown pumpkins the original flavour is always the best.

1 tablespoon olive oil
2 onions, peeled and chopped
1 medium butternut pumpkin,
    peeled, seeded and chopped
1 medium potato, peeled and chopped
4-6 cups vegetable stock
nutmeg
sour cream for serving
finely chopped chives

In a heavy-based soup pot heat the olive oil and sauté the onions until soft and translucent. Add the pumpkin and potato and stir for a minute before pouring in the stock. Bring to the boil then turn down to simmer and cook until the vegetables are soft. You can put this through a food processor in batches (allow it to cool a bit first) or simply use a potato masher to blend it all together. I prefer the latter because it's chunkier, but some people like a smooth, creamy soup. Grate a little nutmeg in before serving and garnish with a teaspoon of sour cream and a sprinkling of chives.
cooking time 1 hour • serves 4-6

The Long Table

The delight of coming home to soup heating on the wood stove.

Tomato and basil soup

French toast

Afternoon tea

During the Leura years my mother made a point of preparing a good afternoon tea for the children when they arrived home from school. There was always fruit in the bowl, and the boys also often made themselves a sandwich (or two) as they grew into their teens. But Mum also made sweet treats for them and their memories of this afternoon ritual are treasured.

French toast

This is a quick filler for after school and a great way of using up stale bread and excess eggs. It's also good for breakfast and sometimes as a late supper before going to bed.

4 eggs, lightly whisked
2 tablespoons milk
salt and pepper
1 teaspoon butter for frying
8 slices of bread with the crusts removed

Combine the beaten eggs and milk and season with salt and pepper. Melt butter in a heavy-based frying pan until it bubbles – avoid letting it smoke or turn brown. Dip the bread in the egg mixture, allowing the excess to drip back into the bowl, then lay flat in the frying pan – it should cook until brown and slightly crisp, about 4 minutes each side.
cooking time 8-10 minutes • serves 4

Pikelets, jam and cream

1½ cups self raising flour, sifted
¼ teaspoon baking powder
1 tablespoon melted butter
3 tablespoons raw sugar
¾ cup full cream milk
1 egg
extra butter for cooking

Sift the flour and baking powder together into a mixing bowl. Mix the melted butter with the sugar and milk. Lightly whisk the egg, but avoid making it frothy. Make a well in the centre of the flour and using a wire whisk combine the flour, egg and milk mixtures. It should make a smooth batter that is not too thick – it needs to be able to drop off the spoon into the pan. Let the batter sit for 30 minutes then melt butter in a good frying pan until it bubbles. Each pikelet should be about a tablespoon of batter or slightly less. They will form a neat circle and should be cooked for a few minutes until the batter starts to bubble on top, then flipped and cooked for several more minutes until brown. Allow them to cool before serving with jam and whipped cream.
cooking time 15 minutes • serves 4

Scones

Although easy, scones do require a 'light touch' or they will be heavy and chewy. The trick is to preheat the oven and handle the dough as little as possible so it is mixed, cut and popped into the oven within a few minutes. Speed is of the essence.

2 cups plain flour, sieved
1 tablespoon baking powder
pinch of salt
30g butter, chopped into small squares
½ tablespoon caster sugar
¾ cup full cream milk
extra milk for glazing

Sieve the flour, baking powder and salt together and quickly, by hand, rub the butter into the flour until it resembles fine breadcrumbs. Add the caster sugar and then lightly mix in the milk, again by hand, to form a dough that is soft but not sticky. Add more flour if necessary. Turn onto a floured board, making a round shape that is about 3-4 cm thick. Use a scone cutter dipped in flour to cut the dough, starting from the middle and working outwards. Leftover dough can be pulled together and cut into the last few scones. Place the scones onto a greased baking tray so they are just touching each other then using a pastry brush, lightly brush with milk. Immediately put into a preheated hot oven (220°) and cook for 12-15 minutes until the scones are golden brown. Serve while still hot – break the scones in half rather than cutting them – and serve with jam and whipped cream. My husband puts butter on as well as the jam and cream which is why I no longer make scones very often.

cooking time 12-15 minutes • serves 6

Mum's scones were as light as a feather.

Life for the children was uncomplicated. Homework was done at the kitchen table when the afternoon tea was finished, then they were free to play outside until dinnertime. They loved the fruit trees and often helped at harvest time – Aaron picking peaches in the summer.

Main courses

After breakfast and getting the children off to school Mum and I would sit at the kitchen table with a cup of tea and plan the evening meal. She liked to be organised well in advance and would often get started on preparing the vegetables and building up the fire in the wood stove while I was at my desk writing.

Fish stew

This recipe was taught to me by a French/Australian friend – Richard D'Erceville – who in turn learned the secret from his mother. The first time we made it together was at our beach house in Jervis Bay using local fish and it has become one of our family staples, known affectionately as the Dick D'Erceville Stew. The grandchildren ask for it, by that name, at least once a week.

2 tablespoons good olive oil

2 onions, peeled and finely chopped

2 cloves garlic, peeled and minced

1 large tomato, peeled and chopped

1kg waxy potatoes, peeled and chopped into chunks

4 carrots, peeled and sliced

6 saffron threads dissolved in ¼ cup boiling water

1-2 litres fish stock

salt and pepper

1-1.5kg fish (mix bone-free varieties including salmon, perch and flathead), chopped into bite-sized chunks

parsley, finely chopped for serving

fish stock

1-2 litres cold water

1 fish head

bay leaf

4 black peppercorns

stick of celery, including foliage

½ onion, roughly chopped

The aim of this soup/stew is to combine different types of fish flesh in a rich stew of stock and vegetables. Like all recipes where only one cooking pot is involved, it relies on the wonderful exchange of flavours.

The fish stock can be made the same day because unlike meat or chicken stock, there is no fat to be skimmed off.

To make the stock, put the water, fish head and other ingredients into a soup pot. Bring to the boil and simmer for 20 minutes only – any longer and the stock will become bitter. Strain through a colander and set aside.

In the same pot heat the olive oil and sauté the onions until they become lovely and soft and translucent. Add the garlic and stir, then the chopped tomato. On a low heat allow these ingredients to blend together so that their flavours really emerge – I stir them with a wooden spoon every few minutes for at least 10 minutes. Add the potatoes and carrots and stir so they are well coated with the tomato/onion mix. Add saffron and pour over the stock and bring to the boil. Turn down and simmer gently until the potatoes and carrots are cooked. Season with salt and black pepper, throw in the fish and cook for 5 minutes (or until fish is cooked but not falling apart). Serve in deep bowls, sprinkled with finely chopped parsley, accompanied by crunchy brown bread and butter.

• You can use commercially prepared fish stock (watered down) if time is short.

• I sometimes add 500g of peeled green prawns with the fish, just to make it a bit different.

cooking time 1 hour • serves 6-8

Roast chicken with stuffing

When I was a child chicken was a luxury, but these days it's the least expensive meat and therefore cooked often. Cheap mass–produced chickens are waterlogged and when roasted this swamps the cooking pan and makes the potatoes soggy. Therefore I recommend roasting corn fed, free range or organic chickens.

1 medium size free range or organic chicken
2 tablespoons olive oil
soy sauce
salt and pepper
1kg potatoes, peeled, chopped and parboiled for
    5 minutes
stuffing
½ tablespoon butter
1 onion, peeled and chopped
1 rasher lean bacon, rind removed and chopped
4 slices stale bread, crumbed in a food processor
sprinkling of mixed herbs (or fresh herbs)
salt and pepper

To make the stuffing, melt the butter in a heavy-based frying pan and sauté the onion until soft. Add the bacon and cook for a few more minutes, then allow to cool slightly before adding the breadcrumbs, herbs and salt and pepper.

Rinse the chicken under cold water and dry with paper towel, including the inside. Spoon the stuffing into the bird – it should fill the cavity but not be jammed in too tightly or it will get soggy in the cooking. Use skewers to secure the stuffing hole and then massage soy sauce and a little olive oil into the skin. Season all over with salt and pepper. Preheat the oven to 200º. Place the chicken in a baking dish with the olive oil, breast side down and place in the oven. After 5 minutes the pan should start to sizzle. Use a fork to move the bird around in the pan to make sure the breast skin isn't sticking. This way the juices run down into the breast meat, keeping it moist. Baste the bird every 15 minutes with the juices from the pan. After 30 minutes add the parboiled potatoes, and continue basting and turning the potatoes until 10 minutes before the bird is cooked, when it can be turned over to allow the breast skin to brown and crisp. After 1 hour and 20 minutes take out the chicken and allow it to rest for 15 minutes, covered.

Turn up the oven to 220º and put the roasting pan with the potatoes on the top shelf to get crispy. Lift them onto a clean baking tray and keep in the oven, while making gravy from the pan juices (see page 35).
cooking time 1½ hours • serves 4-6

Slow cooked beef casserole

This is a basic recipe which can be varied enormously – bacon can be added, or parsnips or mushrooms. Anything you like. I like to cook it the day before because the flavours develop overnight, making it even more tasty. I also make more than is required because it's great on toast for breakfast the following day.

1 tablespoon plain flour
salt and pepper
1.5kg chuck steak, trimmed of fat and cut into large
    chunks
2 tablespoons olive oil
1 large or 2 small brown onions, peeled and chopped
2 cloves of garlic, peeled and mashed
1 tablespoon tomato paste
½ cup red wine
4 cups stock
3 large carrots, peeled and sliced

Put the flour, salt and pepper into a plastic bag. Add the meat and shake so it is entirely coated. Heat the oil in a heavy-based casserole (one that can be used on a cook top then transferred into the oven). Sauté the onions until soft and translucent then add the garlic and cook for a further 3 minutes. Lift out the onion and garlic and, if necessary, add a little extra oil. Brown the meat in batches – shaking off excess flour. Return the onions and meat to the pan and add the tomato paste, coating the meat and cooking for a few minutes. Add the wine, stock (see page 32) and carrots. Bring to the boil then transfer to a low-moderate oven (160º) and cook slowly for 1½-2 hours.

I check after an hour of cooking and add more water if the stew is looking dry. The following day I reheat, also very slowly, and serve with mashed potatoes or rice and a salad.
cooking time 2 hours • serves 6

Roast chicken with stuffing

A light brush of egg yolk to glaze.

Chicken and mushroom pie

There are two ways of making this pie – one with a béchamel (milk-based) sauce; and one with a roux (stock-based) sauce. I prefer the latter because it is more subtle and uses the stock in which the chicken has been cooked.

1 free range or corn fed chicken
6-8 black peppercorns
1 stick of celery with leaves
½ onion, peeled
1 carrot, peeled
bay leaf
2 tablespoons butter
1 onion, peeled and sliced
300g field mushrooms, sliced
1 tablespoon plain flour
salt and pepper
shortcrust pastry (see page 43)
egg yolk for glazing

Cook the chicken and make the stock the day before. In a soup pot put the chicken, peppercorns, celery, onion, carrot and bay leaf and cover with water. Bring to the boil and simmer for 30 minutes. Lift the chicken and set aside. Strain the stock through a sieve then refrigerate overnight. When the chicken has cooled remove the skin and break the meat into bite-sized chunks, then also refrigerate overnight.
Skim the fat from the stock. In a heavy-based frying pan melt 1 tablespoon of butter and sauté the onion until soft. Add the mushrooms and continue to cook, adding a little extra butter if necessary. Set aside. Melt 1 tablespoon of butter in the same pan, stir in the flour, cooking gently for 2 minutes to remove the floury taste. Gradually add the chicken stock, stirring constantly with a wooden spoon, until you have a smooth sauce. Add the chicken, mushrooms and onion and set aside to cool. Season with salt and pepper.
Line a buttered pie dish with half the rolled-out pastry. Fill with the cooled chicken mixture and top with more rolled-out pastry. Seal the edges with a fork and lightly glaze the top with egg yolk, pricking several holes in the top with the fork. Put into a hot oven (220°) for 45 minutes until the pastry is browned. Serve with mashed potatoes and beans with butter and garlic.
cooking time 1½ hours • serves 4-6

Shepherd's pie

On a cold winter's evening there is nothing more popular than this old fashioned mince and potato pie. I recently had my four grandsons from Adelaide for the school holidays and the night they arrived with their dad, exhausted from the long journey, two enormous serving dishes of shepherd's pie disappeared in about 15 minutes – even the crust around the edge of the dishes was picked off.

1 tablespoon olive oil
2 onions, peeled and finely chopped
1.5kg mixed mince (lean beef, pork, veal or lamb)
1 teaspoon dark soy sauce
1 tablespoon Worcestershire sauce
1 tablespoon gravy flour
water
salt and pepper
1kg mashing potatoes, peeled and cut into chunks
¾ cup milk
2 tablespoons butter

Heat the oil in a heavy-based frying pan and sauté the onions until soft and transluscent. Lift and set aside. Add more oil if necessary and fry the mince at high heat in two batches – the aim is to brown it as much as possible. Use a wooden spoon to break the chunks up, producing a fine, even mince. Add the soy and Worcestershire sauce and stir a little more. Add the gravy flour and cook for 5 minutes before covering the meat with water and turning down the heat to a low simmer. Season with salt and pepper. Put a lid on the pan and cook for 25 minutes. Meanwhile put the potatoes in a pot of boiling water and cook through. Strain, allowing the potatoes to dry out before returning them to the pot (off the heat). Mash thoroughly, then add milk and butter and keep mashing until all the lumps have gone. Put the mince into an ovenproof dish then top with the mashed potato, using a fork to create a smooth top. Cook in a moderate oven (200°) for a further 20 minutes, or until the potatoes are brown on top and the mince is bubbling away underneath.
cooking time 50 minutes • serves 6-8

Spinach pie

I can't remember how many times I made this during the Seventies and Eighties – perhaps once a week – I had such a lot of silver beet in the garden, as well as an oversupply of fresh eggs, so it was a logical solution. It was also very fashionable at the time – it's based on a Greek recipe called Spanakopita, and although it's quite fiddly it's definitely worth the effort.

2 tablespoons olive oil
1 onion, peeled and chopped
1½ bunches of silver beet, washed and chopped
200g good fetta cheese, chopped
200g ricotta cheese
small sprig mint, chopped finely
3 eggs, lightly beaten
salt and pepper
10 sheets of filo pastry
½ cup olive oil

Lightly oil a baking tray that is about the size of a filo pastry sheet.
Defrost the filo pastry sheets but keep them between two lightly moist tea towels or they will dry out. In a deep frying pan heat the olive oil and lightly sauté the onions, until they are soft and translucent. Add the chopped silver beet and stir with a wooden spoon until it wilts and softens. Allow to cool slightly. In a large mixing bowl put the silver beet and onions, the cheeses, the chopped mint and the eggs then combine thoroughly by hand. Season with salt and pepper. Place a sheet of pastry in the baking tray then brush with oil, repeating until you have 5 layers of pastry. Place the pie filling on top and then cover with another 5 layers of pastry, each one brushed with oil. Brush the final layer with oil and sprinkle with freshly grated black pepper and bake in a moderate (170º) oven for 45 minutes – it should be golden brown on top. Allow the pie to set for 5 minutes before serving.
cooking time 45 minutes • serves 6-8

Spaghetti and meatballs

I make my own rich tomato sauce for pasta by roasting home grown tomatoes in the oven with a few other vegetables. This can be served alone or added to mince for regular bolognaise, or used as a base with spicy meatballs for something a little more special.

sauce
2kg tomatoes, roughly chopped
6 cloves of garlic
2 carrots, peeled and sliced
2 onions, peeled and chopped
1 red capsicum, roughly chopped
salt and pepper
small bunch of basil, chopped
2 tablespoons olive oil
meatballs
1 slice of stale bread
⅓ cup milk
1kg veal and pork mince
1 egg
1 onion, peeled and finely chopped
2 teaspoons finely chopped parsley
½ teaspoon hot chilli sauce
1 teaspoon mustard

To make the sauce, put all the ingredients into a shallow roasting pan, mixing the oil through the vegetables by hand. Roast in a moderate (170º) oven for 1 hour, checking regularly to make sure the sauce isn't burning – use a wooden spoon to stir it. The sauce should thicken and slightly caramelise. Allow this to cool before putting through a food processor.
For the meatballs, put the bread and milk into a mixing bowl and allow the bread to soften. Add all the other ingredients and mix thoroughly by hand. Each meatball should be about the size of a heaped tablespoon. They can either be cooked in a non-stick frying pan until brown on all sides, or in the oven for 20 minutes on a lightly greased baking tray, turning once.
Heat the tomato sauce and if it's too thick, add a little red wine and some extra water. Add the meatballs and simmer for a few minutes before serving over cooked pasta. Shaved Parmesan cheese, of course, is a great way to finish off this meal.
cooking time 1½ hours • serves 4-6

The house had three fires – the wood stove in the kitchen, an open fireplace in the living room and a slow combustion stove in the glassed-in verandah. It was always cosy, even during the coldest winter.

Scalloped potatoes

This is a heavenly dish that depends on very thinly sliced potatoes and slow cooking for its success. Look for floury potatoes (the ones that are recommended for mashing) as these will absorb with milk and cream much better. It's the original French comfort food.

butter for greasing the baking dish
300ml pouring cream
1 cup milk
2kg potatoes, peeled and sliced as thinly as possible
salt
grated black pepper
1 teaspoon butter

Lightly grease a shallow baking dish with butter. Combine the cream and milk in a jug. The idea is to layer the potatoes in the baking dish, pouring the milk and cream mixture between each layer and seasoning each layer with salt and pepper. The top should be brushed with the remaining milk, seasoned and the butter divided into five or six dabs – it will melt and help to brown the top. Put in a low (150°) oven and cook slowly so that all the milk and cream are absorbed and the top is crispy and brown. Serve with roasted meat, grilled lamb chops or a fillet of beef.

• There are many variations of this. Some people grate cheese between the layers (as well as the milk) or add two lightly beaten eggs to the milk to create an entirely different consistency. All are delicious.

cooking time 1¼-1½ hours • serves 6-8

There were often parties in the kitchen. Here former Senator Jim McClelland in deep discussion with my workmates Jane Edmanson and Peter Cundall from ABC *Gardening Australia* days.

Sunday night

This was the one night of the week when I relaxed our rule about sitting at the table. There was usually soup followed by something quick and easy and I encouraged the children to get involved in cooking and serving themselves.

Jaffles

If you don't have an open fire and an old-fashioned jaffle iron, simply make these toasted treats in a sandwich maker. The range of fillings is endless.

sliced bread (square)
butter
filling
salt and pepper

The bread must be buttered on the outside so that it doesn't stick to the jaffle iron and also because the butter will help the bread to become brown and crisp. Don't overfill each sandwich or the contents will squeeze out. Place one slice of bread on the bottom, add several tablespoons of filling or layer the ham and cheese and tomato (or whatever) then place a slice of bread on the top, butter side up. Squeeze the jaffle iron together and cook for 10 minutes – a little longer if you peek and the toast hasn't turned lovely and brown.
cooking time 10-15 minutes

Spanish omelette

This is my own variation on the simple, classic omelette from Spain which usually has just onions, garlic and potatoes as the basis. I bulk mine up with lots of vegetables and some bacon or chorizo sausage which makes it a more hearty meal for a hungry family.

3 medium size potatoes, peeled and halved
2 onions, peeled and chopped
2 tablespoons olive oil
4 cloves garlic, crushed
4 rashers of bacon, rind removed and chopped
    (or 2 chorizo sausages, sliced thinly)
1 red capsicum, diced
8 eggs, beaten
¼ cup milk
salt and pepper
pinch cayenne pepper
¼ teaspoon chilli flakes
2 tomatoes, sliced thinly

Parboil the potatoes for 10-12 minutes. Allow them to cool slightly. In a cast-iron or ovenproof frying pan sauté the onions in the olive oil until soft and translucent, adding the garlic towards the end. Now add the bacon (or chorizo) and continue to cook until brown but not crisp. Slice the potatoes and add them to the mix, allowing them to cook some more and become a little brown from the onion bacon mix. When they seem cooked through add the capsicum and pour over the combined eggs and milk. Season with salt, pepper, cayenne and chilli. On the lowest possible heat let the omelette cook until it appears partially set. Arrange tomatoes on the surface of the omelette. Put the pan under a hot grill – the omelette will puff up and turn a lovely golden brown. Test with a knife to ensure there are no runny eggs still inside and allow to set for 5 minutes before serving.
cooking time 25 minutes • serves 4-6

Spanish omelette

Ishmael's influence

In 1984 we were visited by international filmmaker Ishmael Merchant, who was in Australia to work with my husband David on a film. Ishmael was born in Mumbai (Bombay) in India and made his name with some hugely popular films. Sadly he died in 2005. Ishmael was famous not just as a filmmaker, but as an inspired cook – he cooked us some wonderful meals. I would follow him around our unsophisticated kitchen and take notes as he cooked, drank wine and told anecdotes from his life in film.

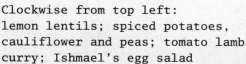

Clockwise from top left:
lemon lentils; spiced potatoes,
cauliflower and peas; tomato lamb
curry; Ishmael's egg salad

Lemon lentils

1 cup vegetable oil
2 medium onions, halved and thinly sliced
4 cinnamon sticks
1kg masoor dal (lentils), washed and drained
1 tablespoon chopped fresh ginger
5 cups chicken stock
1 teaspoon cayenne pepper
1 lemon, juiced (plus the skin, chopped)
1 small onion peeled
1 garlic clove, peeled and chopped
1 hot green chilli, chopped with seeds
4 bay leaves
2 tablespoons fresh coriander leaves, chopped
salt

Heat ¾ cup of the oil in a large, heavy-based saucepan and sauté the onions, cooking slowly, until they soften. Add the cinnamon, lentils and ginger and stir for 10 minutes. Add the stock and about 4 cups of water and bring to the boil. Season with salt and cayenne pepper. Add the lemon juice and pieces of chopped lemon skin and cook for about 50 minutes, stirring every so often to ensure it doesn't stick to the base of the pan. In a small frying pan heat the rest of the oil and fry the rest of the chopped onion, garlic, chilli and bay leaves. Stir until onion is cooked and brown. At the time of serving add this mixture to the lentils and garnish with coriander leaves.
cooking time 1½ hours • serves 6-8

92

Ishmael's egg salad

1 tablespoon mayonnaise
1 tablespoon Dijon mustard
1 green chilli, seeded and chopped finely
2 spring onions, finely chopped
10 hardboiled eggs, peeled and quartered
salt and pepper

Mix the mayonnaise, mustard, chilli and spring onions together. Pour over chopped eggs and toss lightly. Season with salt and pepper.
cooking time 10 minutes • serves 4

Tomato lamb curry

¼ cup vegetable oil
3 bay leaves, crushed
1 cinnamon stick
2 cloves
4 cardamon pods
4 peppercorns
1kg boneless lamb meat, cubed
1 large onion, peeled and chopped
½ teaspoon ground ginger
2 cloves garlic, peeled and chopped
¼ teaspoon turmeric
½ teaspoon ground coriander
1 teaspoon chilli powder
salt
1 large tomato, peeled and chopped
1 tablespoon fresh coriander, chopped

Heat the oil in a heavy-based saucepan. Sauté the bay leaves, cinnamon, cloves, cardamon pods and peppercorns until they begin to pop – 2-3 minutes. Add the lamb and the onion, cooking until slightly brown. Stir in the ginger, garlic, turmeric, ground coriander, chilli powder and salt. Cook for a further 5 minutes on medium before adding the tomato. Keep cooking until the tomato softens then add 2 cups of hot water. Cover the pan, turn to low heat and simmer for 1 hour until the meat is tender. Garnish with fresh coriander before serving.
cooking time 1¼ hours • serves 4-6

Spiced potatoes, cauliflower and peas

¼ cup vegetable oil
2 medium onions, peeled and chopped
2 cloves garlic, peeled and crushed
¼ teaspoon turmeric
½ teaspoon cayenne pepper
12 black peppercorns
6 medium-sized potatoes, peeled and sliced
½ cauliflower, cut into florets
½ teaspoon salt
2 green chillies, seeded and chopped
¼ cup lemon juice
1½ cups frozen peas

In a heavy-based cooking pot heat the oil and sauté the onions, garlic, turmeric, cayenne pepper and peppercorns for 10 minutes, stirring occasionally. Add the potatoes and cauliflower and stir until well coated with spices. Add salt, lemon juice, chillies and 1 cup of hot water. Turn the heat to low and cover the saucepan, cooking slowly for 25 minutes. Add the peas and cook for a further 5-10 minutes.
cooking time 45 minutes • serves 6-8

Desserts

Desserts were reserved for special occasions and not served routinely after every meal because in those days young mothers were concerned about feeding children too much sugar. So when we did have dessert it was considered a real treat.

Summer pudding

In Leura we grew lots of fresh berries and currants and in spring and summer it was hard to keep up with the harvesting to make the most of the yield. This was always a favourite way to use the fruit, although the children also liked to just graze while they were playing.

2 tablespoons caster sugar
¼ cup cold water
¼ teaspoon vanilla essence (or scraped half pod of vanilla bean)
1kg mixed fresh berries (raspberries, blackberries, blueberries, red or black currants)
small loaf white bread, sliced with crusts removed

In a heavy-based saucepan place the water, sugar and vanilla and heat until the sugar has dissolved. Add the fruit and bring back to the boil, then remove immediately from the heat (or the berries will disintegrate). Allow to cool. Line a pudding bowl with slices of white bread (cover the base and sides). Pour the fruits into the mould and then cover the top with more slices of white bread, cutting them to fit neatly. Cover with plastic wrap then use a small plate or saucer (smaller than the top of the bowl) to weigh it down. You can put a can of tuna (unopened) on the top as an extra weight. If it stays overnight in the refrigerator it will set and should be unmoulded (turned upside down) onto a cool plate and served immediately, with whipped cream.
cooking time 10 minutes • serves 4-6

Pavlova

There isn't a dessert I have made as often as this – my sons and grandsons are addicted – not to mention David. We are lucky to have a good supply of fresh eggs, and strawberries in the summer. I made it for my sister's friends in Canada and they were enchanted.

4 eggs whites
1½ cups caster sugar
1 teaspoon cornflour
a few drops of vanilla essence
1 teaspoon white vinegar
300ml pure cream
1 punnet strawberries
2 bananas
2 kiwi fruit
3 passionfruit

Preheat oven to 180°. Grease a pizza tray and cover it with baking paper, also greased. Whisk the egg whites until they are firm and form peaks. Gradually add the sugar – half a tablespoon at a time – so that it is completely absorbed by the eggs whites. At the end beat (slowly) the cornflour, vanilla and vinegar into the mix. Use a spatula to pile the meringue onto the pizza tray – it should be about as round as a dinner plate and about 10 cm high. Put into the preheated oven and immediately turn the temperature down to 140°. Cook slowly for 45-50 minutes, longer if you want a more crunchy meringue. Turn the oven off and leave the pavlova shell inside until the oven is completely cool. Whip the cream and spread over the top of the meringue. Top with sliced strawberries, bananas and kiwi fruit and finally scoop the pulp of the passionfruit over the fruit. Serve immediately.
cooking time 50 minutes-1 hour • serves 6-8

Glazed pears

Getting good pears is difficult. They are picked under ripe and seem to go from rock solid to rotten overnight. The solution is to cook them as a dessert while still firm – almost ripe but not quite.

4 teaspoons butter, melted
8 pears, peeled
1-2 tablespoons caster sugar
4 tablespoons water
1 vanilla pod, scraped
whipped pure cream for serving

Grease a shallow ceramic ovenproof dish with butter. It must be large enough so that the pears can fit neatly in one layer. Brush pears with melted butter and sprinkle with the sugar. Put the water and the scraped vanilla pod into the base of the dish. Cover the dish with aluminium foil and put into a preheated oven (160º). The idea is to cook the pears slowly for one hour. Baste them every 15 minutes with the juices and check they are tender with a skewer, giving them a little longer in the oven if necessary. Turn the oven up to 200º and remove the foil. Cook for a further 15 minutes to brown and slightly caramelise the fruit. Serve warm with whipped cream.

cooking time 1¼ hours • serves 8

Fresh
ingredients
and simplicity.

The road through
parenthood is long
and hard, and as we
have discovered some
36 years later,
never-ending.

Walnut charlotte

Bread and butter pudding

This is a rich dessert but it's a good way of using up stale bread. The marmalade glaze is an optional extra. I have also eaten this pudding made with prune spread instead of butter. If you choose to do this, omit the currants.

50g butter
12 slices white bread, crusts removed
50g dried currants
4 eggs
4 egg yolks (use the whites for pavlova)
150g caster sugar
300ml pure cream
300ml thickened cream
1 scraped vanilla pod
2 tablespoons fine orange marmalade

Grease the inside of a heatproof ceramic baking dish. Butter the slices of bread and cut in half (triangles). Line the baking dish with the bread then layer the bread to fill the dish, sprinkling the currants between each layer. Whisk the eggs, yolks and sugar together until light and frothy. In a heavy-based saucepan put the creams and the vanilla from the pod and heat until scalding point (do not allow to boil). Pour the cream into the egg mixture, using a wire whisk to combine evenly. Strain this mixture into the baking dish, covering the bread. Let the pudding settle for 10 minutes then place in large baking dish half filled with water. This needs to go into a preheated oven (180º) for 30 minutes (it might be a good idea to loosely cover the top of the pudding with aluminium foil for the first 15 minutes to prevent the top from browning too much). Melt the marmalade in a small saucepan for 2 minutes then glaze the top of the pudding with a pastry brush. Return to the oven for a further 3-5 minutes to produce a golden topping.

cooking time 45 minutes • serves 4-6

Walnut charlotte

¾ cup caster sugar
¾ cup boiling water
1 tablespoon walnut liqueur (or brandy)
12 sponge finger biscuits
250g softened butter
300g walnut pieces, finely chopped
2 tablespoons dark rum
6 egg whites
1 cup ripe raspberries (or blackberries)

Make a sugar syrup by mixing half the sugar into the boiling water and simmer for a few minutes. Add the walnut liqueur. Line the sides and base of a terrine dish with the biscuits and pour this mixture evenly over them. Now mix together the butter, walnuts and rum. Whip the egg whites until they are stiff and form peaks, adding the remainder of the sugar until well absorbed. Fold this into the butter/walnut mix until well combined. Pour into the terrine, tapping down well so there are no air pockets. Chill for at least 3 hours and serve with the berries.

serves 4-6

Family recipes

97

Creamy zucchini soup (recipe p125)

Almost every meal starts with a bowl of soup.

France

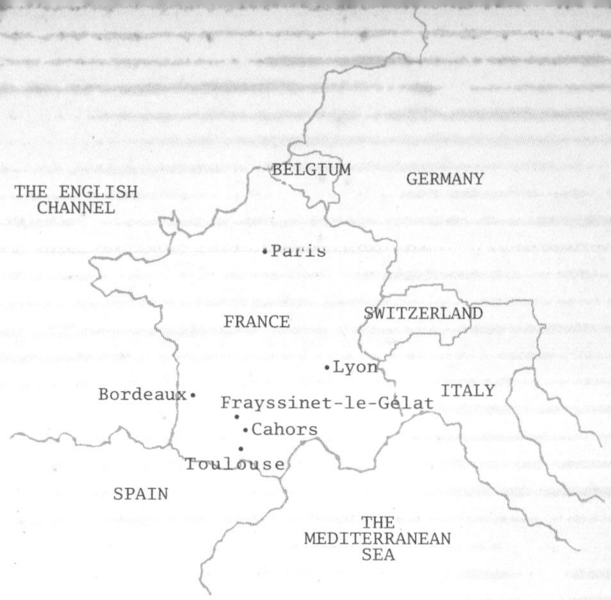
BELGIUM
GERMANY
THE ENGLISH CHANNEL
Paris
FRANCE
SWITZERLAND
Lyon
Bordeaux
Frayssinet-le-Gélat
ITALY
Cahors
Toulouse
SPAIN
THE MEDITERRANEAN SEA

The family gradually

grew smaller as each of the children left home to further their education. My love of gardening had an influence as our sons Aaron and Ethan opted to study horticulture. Our daughter Miriam went to university in Canberra and the oldest, Tony, took an apprenticeship in Sydney.

With the house at Leura empty I suddenly felt an overwhelming urge to escape, to spread my wings and have some time to myself. David was shooting two feature films in Queensland so I packed my bags and went on my own to France where I rented a small room in the back of a shop in a medieval fortified township (bastide) just inside the border of the Dordogne. I spent six delightful months being totally irresponsible and discovering the joys of French rural life.

I had never lived alone before and it was a glorious feeling, waking up every morning and wondering 'what will I do today?' After years of juggling working full-time, rearing a boisterous family and maintaining a large house and garden, suddenly having 'free' time was a total luxury. Sometimes I'd wake and then just roll over and go back to sleep. And sometimes I would get in my beat up old Peugeot and drive around the French countryside, soaking up each beautiful scene.

So many aspects of French life appeal to me, regardless of the season. The people, the architecture, the markets laden with fresh produce and of course the food and wine. Everywhere you look is a feast for the eyes.

I never tire of walking through
the villages and I am particularly
attracted to the old,
abandoned stone houses that hold
memories of the familes
who once lived there.

My kitchen is small but designed
for easy food preparation.
Although I sometimes shop in
supermarkets, I prefer fresh
produce from the local markets
and, like the locals, I shop
almost every day.

It's fun to scour the flea markets and antique stalls for old kitchen utensils and crockery. Over the years I have found wonderful cooking pots, china and glasses.

In the beginning I was quite timid about the food. Language skills (or lack of them) were a factor. I made mistakes. My first blunder was ordering choucroute at a large and crowded restaurant in Cahors one Sunday lunchtime. It was the speciality of the house but I had absolutely no idea what it was: I recognised pomme de terre (potato) and saucisse (sausage) and foolishly believed I couldn't go far wrong with those two ingredients. When the meal arrived it was on a huge serving platter – enough to feed four people. There were boiled potatoes all right, plus seven different types of cooked sausage, arranged on a steaming mound of hot, spicy sauerkraut. It was quite tasty but so enormous that I was daunted and hardly ate a thing. The waiter looked offended and I scurried out leaving rather a large tip.

My first friend in France was Jock Veitch, a retired journalist originally from New Zealand who I had known briefly in Sydney in the 1970s when we had worked for the same publisher. Now in his seventies, Jock lives comfortably in the charming small village of St. Caprais, just inside the Departement du Lot.

Jock loves to talk – he's a natural raconteur – and to drink gallons of wine. But most of all he loves to eat and under his tutelage I embraced French rural cuisine and gained 12 kilos into the bargain. Jock introduced me to Croque Monsier, a toasted cheese and ham sandwich that oozes cholesterol; to salade de gesiers, a mixture of green leaves, toasted walnuts and sautéed preserved duck's gizzards; and to eau de vie, a local drink made from plums or pears that is stronger than rocket fuel and should only be sipped with the greatest of caution. I discovered the belief that 'French women don't get fat' is totally untrue.

France

The room is flooded with light from the arched windows.

The kitchen is at one end of
the main downstairs room, like
so many French rural houses.
Where the kitchen is located
now was once a shop, opening
onto the busy main road.

The houses along the main roads of
Frayssinet are built with such
narrow footpaths that most villagers
walk in the street when coming and
going from the boulangerie.

a small
in the
back of a shop
in a medieval
fortified towns
(bastide) just
inside the bord
of the Dordogr
I spent six
delightful mon
being totally
irresponsible a
discovering the

In the kitchen of the restaurant with Gaby, Jeannette Murat and her daughter Sylvie. They work tirelessly to feed a constant stream of hungry workers and local villagers.

Jock also introduced me to a fascinating worker's restaurant in nearby Pomarède that has been owned and operated by five generations of women in the one family for more than 100 years. In rural France there is a strong tradition of manual workers sitting down to a large, hot lunch in the middle of the day.

Jeannette Murat and her daughter Sylvie run the restaurant and on some days they have up to 50 quarry workers and truck drivers and road maintenance crews sitting at their long, polished tables. They only open at midday during the week and then again on Sunday when local families love to come for a special lunch.

The food is not served on plates, instead, each course is brought to the table in a bowl or on a platter so that diners can help themselves. On my first visit I foolishly assumed that we were obliged to eat everything that was offered. I was also unaware that for the modest 12 euros set price we would be given five enormous courses. There is no menu. Each day a different main course (plat) is prepared and diners simply eat whatever is brought to the table. I was with Jock and three others and when we sat down there were two one litre bottles of the local very dark red wine and a small bottle of water in front of us. Amazingly the wine is also included in the cost of the meal.

Within minutes a steaming tureen of soup arrived, and a basket of crusty white bread. The soup was a smooth vegetable broth based on rich veal stock, with fine noodles added. It was delicious but the tureen wasn't emptied and I felt it was good manners to keep eating. I suppose I ate about four slices of bread with my three bowls of soup and was feeling well satisfied. That alone was more than I would normally eat at lunchtime.

Next came two large platters – one with grated and sliced raw vegetables (crudités) and the other a selection of cold meats including local ham (jambon cru) and a rough duck pâté. I used the bread to eat the pâté and to mop up the tasty vinaigrette dressing on the vegetables.

The baker in Frayssinet enjoys
preparing the most elaborate and
unusual gateaux and flans — this
is his version of the traditional
fruit flan with unusual
ingredients such as star fruit,
lychees and kiwi fruit.

The old stone walls inside most houses are warm and inviting. If the stone has been previously rendered, by a process known as crepi, these days it is usually chipped away when the house is renovated.

I am struck by the soft light of France in Autumn and Winter.

By this stage of the meal I was replete. But we weren't even at the halfway mark. We had, however, finished all the wine and two more bottles were instantly delivered. I was having a wonderful time.

Next came a platter of crispy duck legs that were so tender they melted in my mouth. I discovered later this was 'confit du canard' which is a highly prized speciality of the region. Portions of duck were traditionally boiled in goose fat then stored in earthenware jars during winter (in the era before refrigeration). These days you can buy confit freshly made at the markets, or in tins or jars at the supermarket. I struggled through this course, which also included a generous plater of crunchy potatoes and garlic sautéed in goose fat. The red wine continued to be miraculously replenished.

Next came the cheese platter. A wooden board was produced with large slabs of Cantal (a famous cheddar); Roquefort (also famous, a blue cheese made in nearby caves), Camembert and a local soft goat cheese called Cabécou. Plus more bread. By now I realised I didn't HAVE to eat every morsel and therefore had just a fine sliver of each variety.

Lastly dessert. Here we were given a choice of fresh fruit, glace (ice cream), crème brûlée and a fluffy fruit pudding called clafouti. I chose the crème brûlée with its crunchy toffee topping. It was divine. The fact that I could barely move as a result of my gluttony was irrelevant. It was a memorable meal and the first of dozens I have since enjoyed in this welcoming restaurant.

The region of France where I was living during this heady six-month escape, and where I finally bought a small village house, is known as the southwest or Midi Pyrenees. It has remained unspoiled because of its isolation and low population and because it is comparatively poor, like so many rural areas of Europe. Agriculture in the region is heavily subsidised by the French government and in reality it is the only way these farmers can survive. They are immensely proud of the traditional farming culture and history, and this is reflected in the farmers' markets that are held in every small village and township at least once a week.

It's true to say that in France life leads up to lunch. This is why the open markets are always held in the mornings, starting at 8am, and the villagers and folk from surrounding areas come looking for the freshest and tastiest produce they can find. There is a preference for eating seasonally – strawberries and asparagus in the spring; tomatoes and salad greens in the summer; walnuts and mushrooms in the autumn. The locals

The markets are a meeting place where people discuss the freshness of the produce and their favourite seasonal recipes. In the winter the local French language dominates the market square, but by mid-summer English and Dutch and even Australian voices can be heard everywhere.

MIEL ET NOIX
225 g : 3,00 €
450 g : 5,70 €

I was suprised to find such good seafood so far from the coast.

Mussels (moules) are popular throughout France and our local restaurant by the lake serves them every Friday night during summer.

have animated discussions about what's available and the women love to talk about what they are preparing for lunch. It's the most important meal of the day. At noon, sharp, the stallholders pack up and go home because they, too, will be enjoying a proper lunch followed, possibly, by a short sleep.

The markets are a feast for the eye as well as for the stomach. Each stallholder takes great pride in presentation with fruits and vegetables arranged in colourful piles, cold meats and cheeses displayed exquisitely and even the produce at the fish stalls artistically arranged. There are live animals on sale – rabbits and ducks and hens – and there are specialised stalls such as those just selling spices or just offal.

There are supermarkets, of course, and these are also great fun for exploring. Some of the more exotic fresh produce is imported from America or northern Africa, so you can buy mangoes and avocadoes in the winter (unlike the open markets). The cuts of meat are very different and there are foods you simply can't buy in an Australian supermarket. Portions of duck and rabbit and packets of quail are on a cool shelf, along with jars of white goose fat for frying. There are tins of preserved duck and goose liver, and jars of chestnuts and pickled walnuts. Wine can be bought in the supermarket too, and there is an amazing selection in a wide range of prices from the very, very cheap to the ridiculously expensive. Wine is considered part of life in France.

At both the supermarket and the open market there are cheese cabinets displaying a vast array of varieties from all regions of France. It's easy to be daunted by the number of choices. Indeed when I first arrived, I was so overwhelmed that it took me months, with a little help from my friend Claude Luzzatto, to work out my preferred varieties and how to order them. You could, if you wanted to, literally have a different cheese every day for six months!

The church in our village has a lofty tower, which dominates the crossroads. The bell rings on the hour and half hour, all day and right through the night.

My neighbour Claude (below) is an
excellent cook and can talk about food
from dawn till dusk. We meet up for an
evening drink in one of the two village
bars. Here (right) with Claude and Jock.

In my modern kitchen is against a stone wall, and he has managed to squeeze in a refrigerator as well as a dining area. Although the table is small – designed for four to six –

I sometimes leave a meal cooking slowly in the oven while I go to the bar for an evening aperitif. I have to keep a strict eye on the clock – more than once I have returned home to a burnt offering.

The Lot is a great region for mushrooms and truffles, which are highly prized and outrageously expensive. I have never been brave enough to cook with them, but have enjoyed them in omelettes cooked by Jan and once or twice in restaurants when I was feeling extravagant.

I made a lot of friends during my first visit to France and they taught me so much about the local cuisine and customs. I was invited into people's homes which is the best way to learn, especially if you are curious like me. Before lunch or dinner most people serve an aperitif – a small glass of alcohol that is often sweet although a lot of the local men prefer the anise-flavoured pastis (I love it too, but it has quite a punch). Wine is never consumed until after the soup course which makes a lot of sense – not pouring red wine onto an empty stomach!

Some of the older men follow the tradition of chabrol, which involves mixing a quarter of a glass of red wine with the last of the soup in their bowl. This is drunk directly from the bowl and is considered rather 'common' in some circles (I have tried it often and although it sounds revolting, it's absolutely delicious). Green salad is eaten with most meals and the leaves must be folded (never cut with a knife) which is a skill that takes some time to learn. It is quite polite to use bread to mop the plate and bread and butter plates are not provided (the French don't have butter on their bread) and you simply keep your chunk of bread on the table near your plate. Often the same plate, knife and fork are used for several courses – the charcuterie (cold meats) the plat (main course) and the fromage (cheese). Sweet white wine is served with foie gras and cold meats, and again during dessert. Red wine is preferred with the cheese course.

The house that I bought is in the small village of Frayssinet-le-Gélat, and the nearest large town is Cahors which has a wonderful market every Wednesday and Saturday. While not a 'ruin' as so many old buildings are in this region, the house was in desperate need of renovation and during the second year I had new kitchen installed, which made it possible for me, at last, to return some of the kind hospitality of my friends.

Like most old houses in the region the ground floor consists of one large room with a wide open fireplace made of stone where the original inhabitants once would have cooked their meals on the coals. In those days there was no 'living room' furniture as such – no comfortable chairs or sofas. People sat at the table where they talked, then ate, then talked and drank coffee or wine after dinner before going to bed (early). Often the beds were in the same room, some of them folding up and being stored in the corners.

During the early days of the European Union there was talk of introducing strict health regulations, which could have resulted in fresh fruit wrapped in plastic instead of on colourful open display. Fortunately the French objected strongly, although some compromises were made – for example meat and cheese are now displayed under glass.

Me with Philippe and Jan (below);
Margaret Barwick (right) who writes
horticultural books and has the most
spectacular garden; Lucienne and her
granddaughter and me (below right)

Porc au G
du Sud Ouest

1 2 € 0 0

The Lot is the 'duck and goose'
capital of France and local farmers
breed the birds for meat, for
cooking fat and for the delicious
foie gras. The practice is frowned
upon in many countries.

I have made so many friends since living part time in France. Jan and Philippe Claudy (far left) who live in a wonderfully renovated barn; neighbours Morgan and Bill with Trish Hobbs and Dany Chouet who ran the legendry Cleopatra's Guest House in the Blue Mountains for decades.

So in the modern context where we expect a living room as well as a dining area and a kitchen, the space in this one room has to be economically managed. In my house the modern kitchen is against a side wall, and I have managed to squeeze in a refrigerator as well as a dining area. Although the table is small – designed for four to six – I have at times served dinner for 12 by bringing in a table from the courtyard and packing my friends around it. It's very intimate indeed.

Ironically my friends in France are often keen for me to cook Australian-style food; lamb stews, old-fashioned baked dinners and pavlova. I also enjoy cooking them Asian food, which is a bit tricky because I need to travel to Toulouse to get the spices and other ingredients required to make recipes such as chicken laksa or spicy seafood stir fry. Then, when I get back to Australia my family here beg me to cook French food, so I bring back tins of duck confit and jars of foie gras to satisfy their eager taste buds.

My neighbours in the village only speak French and they all welcomed me warmly from the first day I moved in. Those that have a potager (vegetable garden) leave fresh vegetables on my doorstep and I am given walnuts and bottles of wine as gifts when I arrive each year. Last winter one neighbour arrived with a jar of truffles which he had just dug in the nearby woods – I was later informed by another neighbour that the gift was worth hundreds of Australian dollars! I was a little overwhelmed. I believe that in France people work to live rather than live to work. It's a lesson we should all take to our hearts.

France

First courses

Soup is a standard first course in any rural French restaurant, followed by crudités and some sort of preserved meat or a simple salad of regional ingredients. Both courses are usually substantial.

Chabrol

This is a local tradition that goes back centuries but is still practiced today in rural areas. Most French people don't start drinking wine until after the soup (potage) to avoid ingesting alcohol on an empty stomach. Some farmers and workers leave about three tablespoons of soup in the bottom of the bowl then pour in half a glass of red wine. They stir it with the soup spoon then drink it straight from the bowl. It sounds ghastly but I can assure you it's absolutely delicious.

Sylvie's potage

This soup is light and smooth – almost a broth – and is served as the first course most days of the week at restaurant Murat. The flavour is strong but the soup is not filling – just as well because it is followed by four more hearty courses.

2.5-3 litres water
1 veal shank or bone
1 large onion, halved
2 sticks celery, chopped roughly
2 tomatoes, chopped roughly
2 large potatoes, peeled and quartered
3 carrots, peeled and halved
6 cloves of garlic, peeled
salt and pepper
1 cup small vermicelli noodles

This soup is easy because the stock doesn't need to be made in advance. Simply place all the ingredients, except for the vermicelli noodles, into a large soup pot and bring to the boil. Simmer for 1½ hours or slightly more until the vegetables are soft, skimming any froth from the top as it appears. Lift the bone from the soup and allow the stock to cool. You can either strain off the vegetables and just use the stock; or you can force the vegetables through a sieve and return to the stock – this makes a thicker soup. Bring back to a simmer and add the noodles, cooking for a further 15 minutes.
• If there was any fat on the bone you may need to let the stock get cold (in the fridge) before doing the last step because it will need to be skimmed when the fat is solid.
cooking time 2 hours • serves 6-8

Creamy zucchini soup

At restaurant Murat they serve the simple potage (left) most weekdays, but on Sunday they make a special soup, often creamy vegetable. In summer, zucchinis proliferate but don't be tempted to use the ones that have grown into giant marrows because they are watery and tasteless. Instead only use the small, sweet tender ones.

25g unsalted butter
1 onion, peeled and chopped
1 carrot, peeled and chopped
1 stick celery, chopped
1 large potato, peeled and diced
6-8 small zucchinis, sliced
1.5 litres good chicken stock
salt and pepper
2 tablespoons pouring cream (or crème fraîche)

In a large, heavy-based pot melt the butter and sauté the onion until soft and translucent. Add the carrot, celery, potato and zucchini and continue to cook for several minutes, stirring with a wooden spoon. Cover with the stock, bring to the boil and simmer over a low heat for about 1 hour, until all the ingredients are soft. This soup is better strained through a sieve than put through a food processor – it makes it smoother. Force the vegetables through with a wooden spoon but don't return any remaining fibre in the sieve to the pot. Bring back to a simmer and season with salt and pepper, adding the cream before serving. Don't allow it to boil once the cream has been added!
cooking time 1¼ hour • serves 6-8

It's easy to overeat in France if you help yourself to generous portions of every course presented. The trick is to eat just a small portion of everything and always leave room for dessert.

Second course

After soup there is generally a course that includes cold vegetables or salad and some kind of cold meat or pâté or sausage. This is the danger zone where unsuspecting diners eat too much and then feel faint at the sight of a large hot main course.

Salad cabécous

Cabécous is a soft white goat cheese with a powerful aroma and flavour that is quite distinctive. If you can't source it in Australian gourmet shops, look for any soft goat cheese or substitute some slices of Camembert that will respond just as well to toasting.

a bowlful of mixed salad greens, washed and
     spun dry
200g shelled walnuts
150g prosciutto, grilled till crisp and chopped
⅓ cup small pitted black olives
4 slices of baguette, toasted
4 pieces of cabécous (or other soft cheese)
walnut oil dressing
⅓ cup walnut oil
2 teaspoons red wine vinegar
salt and pepper

Toss the salad leaves, walnuts, cooked prosciutto and olives in a bowl with the walnut oil dressing. Divide into four smaller salad bowls. Toast the slices of baguette and top with cheese. Put under a hot grill until cheese starts to melt – just a couple of minutes – and place in the centre of each salad. Serve immediately.

To make the dressing, combine ingredients in a small jar and shake well. Alternatively simply drizzle the walnut oil onto the salad leaves, season with salt and freshly ground black pepper and sprinkle with the juice of ¼ of lemon before serving.

cooking time 2 minutes • serves 4

Ham and melon

This is a traditional second course all over France, and they use sweet rockmelons that are smaller than the varieties we grow, with a smoother green skin. The ham is a local jambon cru, but you can easily substitute prosciutto or pancetta.

1 rockmelon, peeled and sliced
¼ lemon
salt and pepper
500g prosciutto and pancetta
small wedges of cold, unsalted butter
fresh crusty bread

On a platter arrange slices of melon, seasoned with salt and freshly cracked black pepper. Squeeze the lemon over them. Arrange the ham slices so they can be easily served (not stuck together) and decorate with wedges of butter. The tradition is to eat the butter with the ham, accompanied by crusty bread and red wine.

Foie gras

This is the most simple of courses because the foie is already prepared and just needs to be served with toast, some figs and triangles of brown bread toast. In France foie is always served with a sweet white wine – what we would call a dessert wine. The most expensive – and best – is foie gras entire. This is simply the entire liver of a goose or duck that has been cooked unadulterated – it can be bought fresh in France but only tinned or in jars in Australia because the practice of gavage (force feeding) is illegal here. If fresh figs are not in season, look for some confit of fig (or thick fig jam) because the combination of flavours is superb.

Ham and melon

Foie gras

The flavour of food in France is intense because the ingredients are so fresh

Vegetables are more likely to appear in a salad than with the main course (plat).

Salad Nicoise

I have collected egg cups on my travels and taken them home to the farm – my grandchildren each have their favourites.

Salad Niçoise

This is a standard in French cafes yet it is made in several different ways. Sometimes with rice, sometimes with potatoes and always with tinned rather than fresh tuna (although you can substitute if you want to go up-market). This is my own version. You can adjust this according to taste – using fewer potatoes and more tuna.

500g small new potatoes
⅓ cup vinaigrette
250g French beans, top and tailed
425g tin of tuna in salt water (not oil), drained
3 medium tomatoes cut into wedges
100g pitted Kalamata olives
heart of a cos lettuce, washed and dried for serving
4 eggs, hard-boiled and peeled
45g tin of rolled anchovies
2 tablespoons finely chopped parsley
salt and pepper

Boil the potatoes in salted water until cooked – watch them as the skins split easily and they need to be firm or they may disintegrate. Strain and, while hot, cut each in half and sprinkle with vinaigrette – they should soak it all up. Boil the beans in salted water until cooked but still deep green and firm. In a deep bowl combine the warm potatoes, tuna and beans, adding the tomato and olives. Toss lightly. On a serving platter arrange the cos leaves then place the salad in the middle. Decorate with the hard-boiled eggs and anchovies, then garnish with the parsley. Season to taste.

cooking time 15-20 minutes • serves 4

Asparagus and egg salad

In late spring when the asparagus are at their peak in the open markets, this makes a wonderful and light second course. The French prefer to eat seasonally and the flavour of this salad makes it obvious just why they do. Try and get free range eggs, which will have richer, darker yolks.

3 bunches fresh asparagus
1 tablespoon butter
salt and pepper
6 eggs, at room temperature
juice of half a lemon
1 tablespoon finely chopped parsley

Snap the fresh asparagus near the base to remove the tough section of stem. Use a shallow, wide pan that will take the asparagus lying flat. Half fill with water and bring to the boil then slide in the asparagus, cooking for 5-7 minutes (less if they are the very thin variety). Toss in butter and season with salt and pepper while still hot. The eggs should be hardboiled but only for 4½-5 minutes – again depending on the size. The idea is that the whites should be cooked and the yolks still a little bit runny. This salad works best if the asparagus and eggs are still warm – not hot. Arrange the buttered asparagus on a platter, topped by the eggs, which should have been halved. Season eggs with salt and pepper, pour over the lemon juice and garnish with the finely chopped parsley. Use crusty bread to mop up the butter and runny yolks.

cooking time 10-15 minutes • serves 6

French recipes

Duck sausage and crudités

In French markets and supermarkets they sell salami-style sausages made of duck and wild boar meat and it makes an excellent second course served with salad or raw vegetables (crudités). Often the sausage is sliced and simply served with tiny cornichons (dill pickles).

1-2 sausages, sliced
3 carrots, grated or julienned
2 cooked beetroot, cold and sliced thinly
4 ripe tomatoes cut into wedges
3 hard-boiled eggs, halved
salt and pepper
vinaigrette

On a large platter arrange the sausage slices, the grated carrot, beetroot, egg halves and tomato. Season the vegetables and eggs with salt and pepper, and just before taking to the table pour vinaigrette over the carrots and beetroot.
serves 6

Tomato and goat cheese tart

This is often sold in the deli (epicerie) section of the open market and it makes a wonderful second course or light lunch, served with salad. This is an easy version using frozen puff pastry.

1 sheet frozen puff pastry
4 large ripe tomatoes, peeled, seeded and sliced
200g soft white goat cheese, crumbled
⅓ cup finely chopped chives
drizzle of olive oil
salt and pepper
45g can of flat anchovies (optional)

Preheat oven to 220°. Place the pastry sheet on a lightly greased flat baking tray. Cover with tomatoes and crumbled goat cheese. Sprinkle with chives and drizzle over the olive oil. Decorate with anchovies and cook for 20 minutes in the hot oven until the pastry is brown and crisp on the edges and the tomatoes and cheese are bubbling. Serve hot or warm.
cooking time 25 minutes • serves 2

Omelette au cèpes (wild mushrooms)

Cèpes are very much like the Italian porcini – fleshy, creamy yellow mushrooms that are generally harvested in the autumn although I have also seen them in the markets in summer if there has been a cool, wet spell. They have a distinctive flavour that works wonderfully to enhance an omelette, although they are also often added to stews and casseroles.

3 tablespoons of unsalted butter
200g fresh cèpes, finely sliced
1 clove of garlic, finely chopped
1 tablespoon parsley, finely chopped
6 eggs, lightly beaten with salt and pepper

Cèpes need more cooking than most mushroom varieties. Melt 2 tablespoons of the butter in a heavy-based frying pan and add the cèpes, cooking on a low heat for 20 minutes until tender. During the last few moments add the garlic and parsley, and cook a little more – the butter should be well absorbed and there will be some pan juices.
In a non-stick omelette pan melt ½ tablespoon of butter and bring to bubbling point, tipping the pan so the entire surface is covered. Add the eggs, tipping the pan to spread the mixture over the base and up the sides. Use a flat wooden spoon to lift the edges away from the sides so they don't stick. The idea is that the omelette can slip around in the pan and cook half the way through. When it reaches this stage put in the cèpe mixture and cook for another minute, then tip the pan so the omelette slips to one side, folding it over so that it forms a half circle. Slide the omelette onto a warmed serving platter and serve immediately – topped by the remaining butter which will melt. The finished omelette will still be moist in the middle but should be lightly brown on the outside.
cooking time 25 minutes • serves 2

Claude's garden—beautiful even in winter.

The choice of meats, pâté and terrines is vast. In our region many of the cold sausages are made from wild boar or duck, giving them a distinctive local taste.

The cheese stalls at the market can be overwhelming. Many cheeses are made of unpasturised milk giving them a rich, heady aroma and flavour.

Moules marniere (et moules frites)

Moules marniere (et moules frites)

This is my friend Jan's recipe and it is the most delicious version I have ever eaten. It's perfect as a second course or as the main course for a light summer lunch, served with salad and crusty bread. The moules in France are small and sweet – this recipe is not suitable for those large green New Zealand varieties.

1 cup good olive oil
8-10 eschalots, minced
1 bottle white wine (preferably a decent one,
    I use Sevres et Maine muscadet)
black pepper to taste
2kg small mussels, cleaned
1 cup chopped parsley (I use a mixture of curly
    and flat)

Heat the olive oil in a deep saucepan. Gently fry eschalots until transparent. Pour in the wine and bring to the boil. Reduce until about 2 cm left. Add freshly ground pepper, then the mussels and stir well. Put lid on and bring back to boil. Check after 2 minutes and remove opened mussels. Cook for 2 minutes longer, remove opened mussels, discard any that have not opened. Return opened mussels to pan, throw in parsley and stir. Remove from heat and serve. Nowadays these are often served with chips (frites).
• I also put in about 500g of cleaned and sliced encornets (baby calamari) at the same time as the mussles but it is optional. It's really important not to cook them too long or else they become dry and rubbery. You may be shocked at the amount of olive oil but it is the secret to this recipe.
cooking time 30 minutes • serves 4

Roasted preserved duck (confit du canard)

This is the most mouth-watering way that duck is served in southern France. It evolved before refrigeration, when it was necessary to preserve foods to store for eating over the winter. Pieces of duck were boiled in goose or duck fat and then kept in large pottery urns, with lids, covered in the fat. Confit is now available in Australia at good butcher shops and gourmet shops, either in tins or in cryovac packs.

4 pieces of duck confit
salt and pepper

The duck has already been cooked, so the aim is to heat it through and crisp the outside skin, without letting it overcook and dry out. Remove the excess fat and place the pieces, skin side up, into a baking dish and cook for 15 minutes in a preheated oven set at 200°. Alternatively, pan-fry them in a heavy based skillet using the coating of duck fat to cook in. Traditionally the duck is served with potatoes that have been parboiled and also cooked in the duck fat – it's a sensational combination. Serve with green beans steamed and tossed in butter and crushed garlic.
cooking time 15 minutes • serves 4

French recipes

Stuffed quail

Plat

Plat is the French term for main course and in many regional restaurants it changes every day and diners are given no choice – you simply eat what's on offer. The advantage is that it's freshly cooked and on the table quickly.

Grilled duck breast (magret)

This is another classic from the southwest of France and again the trick is to not overcook the breasts of duck – they should be pink and succulent on the inside. If you can't find breast meat look for duck legs – some supermarkets now stock them – and cook in a similar fashion but for slightly less time. They can also be cooked on the barbeque, fat side up for the first 15 minutes, and fat side down for the 5.

4 duck breasts, skin and fat on
2 tablespoons olive oil
salt and pepper

Preheat the grill and rub the duck breasts with olive oil, lightly seasoning them with salt and pepper. Cook the underside of the breast first – for about 15 minutes – test with a skewer because some pink juices should still be flowing. Turn the duck and cook for another 5 minutes or more – the fat will turn brown and crisp and also run down into the breast meat, keeping it moist and tender. Serve with roasted potatoes or frites (potato chips) if you have a deep fryer, and green peas (I use frozen baby peas) or beans tossed in butter.
cooking time 15-20 minutes • serves 4

Stuffed quail

These tender little birds are sold in France with their heads still attached, which makes preparing them a little gruelling for the uninitiated. However they are full of flavour and have very little fat.

4 large quail
500g Italian sausage (in France I use Saussicon de Toulouse)
2 cloves of garlic, peeled and sliced
2 tablespoons olive oil
salt and pepper
4 rashers of bacon (or jambon cru)
cooking string
½ cup red wine
1 tablespoon finely chopped parsley

Remove the heads of the quail. Remove the skins from the sausages. Into each bird put a slice of garlic followed by as much sausage meat as will fit, followed by a second slice of garlic. Rub a little olive oil onto the skin and season with salt and pepper then wrap each bird with the bacon (or jambon) and secure with some cooking string (at a pinch I have used cooking thread, and you can also use small metal skewers). Put the olive oil into a heavy-based pan and brown the birds on the outside, then transfer them to a baking dish. While still hot pour the red wine into the frying pan to deglaze, mixing in all the little crispy bits with a wooden spoon, then pour this over the birds. Cook in a preheated (185°) oven for 25 minutes. Serve with buttered pasta and garnish with finely chopped parsley.
cooking time 35-45 minutes • serves 4

Grilled duck breast (magret)

Each region of France has a specific identity and cuisine. In the Lot the woodland is oak and chestnut and the farm roadsides are planted with walnut trees. Hunters shoot wild boar and deer in autumn and winter and so, along with duck, these basics feature strongly in the markets and on restaurant menus.

Mustard rabbit

This recipe is a simple way of cooking rabbit and the secret is not to overcook the meat because it is low in fat and will become tough very quickly.

1 rabbit, cut into pieces
3 tablespoons Dijon mustard
salt and pepper
2 tablespoons olive oil
½ cup red wine

Coat the rabbit pieces in mustard, season with salt and pepper and allow to stand for at least 3 hours. Preheat the oven to 180° and heat the olive oil in a shallow baking dish in the oven until hot but NOT smoking. Place the rabbit pieces in the hot oil and turn over. Cook for 25-30 minutes only, turning once, and then lift onto a warm serving platter. Put the baking dish on the cook top on a low heat and stir in the red wine to make a tasty sauce. Pour over the rabbit and serve with potatoes in cream (see page 89) and a fresh green salad.
cooking time 30 minutes • serves 4

Cauliflower, tomato and anchovy

This is a tangy way of cooking cauliflower that is a perfect accompaniment to roasted chicken or grilled lamb chops.

½ head cauliflower, cut into florets
2 punnets cherry tomatoes, halved
½ tablespoon unsalted butter
½ tablespoon olive oil
2 x 45g tins anchovies, with the oil drained off
salt and pepper

Cover the cauliflower with salted water and bring to the boil. The aim is to cook the cauliflower but not to overcook it – it should be able to be skewered with a sharp knife but still be firm. Strain and set aside. Stew the tomatoes in the melted butter and olive oil until soft but not mushy. Add the cooked cauliflower and the anchovies. Heat but don't simmer or it may turn mushy. Serve immediately. I combine this with chicken pieces roasted with herbs, garlic and potatoes.
cooking time 20 minutes • serves 4-6 as a side dish

Cassoulet

Cassoulet

This is a labour of love, because of the length of time it takes to prepare and cook, but it's a classic recipe of southwest France. The best I have ever eaten was at the home of Dany Chouet and Trish Hobbs – Dany excelled by using her own confit, just to make it perfect.

500g white beans, soaked in a bowl of water
    overnight
2 onions, peeled
12 cloves (stuck into 1 peeled onion)
bouquet garni – sprig of parsley, thyme and bay leaf
    tied together
salt
1 tablespoon butter
500g salted pork, cut into cubes
500g spicy sausage, cut into 10 cm lengths
4 cloves garlic, peeled and crushed
2 tomatoes, peeled and chopped
6 pieces of duck confit (see note)
salt and pepper
½ teaspoon Herbs de Provence

Drain the water from the beans and cover with fresh water. Add the onion stuck with cloves, the bouquet garni and salt. Cover and cook for 1½ hours or until the beans are about three-quarters cooked. Drain and reserve the liquid. In a heavy-based frying pan melt the butter and brown the salt pork and the sausage. Remove from the pan and use the butter (and pork fat) to sauté the onion, garlic and tomatoes until they all soften and the flavours combine. Simmer this sauce, covered, for 20 minutes. In a large, shallow earthenware casserole spread half the cooked beans and half the tomato sauce then arrange the salt pork, sausage and pieces of duck. Add the rest of the beans and the tomato sauce and pour over some of the bean cooking stock – just to cover the surface. Season with salt and pepper and Herbs de Provence. Bake in a preheated oven (165°) for 2 hours, checking every so often and adding more bean stock if necessary. Remove the lid, turn the oven up to 190° and cook for another 45 minutes, until brown and crisp on top.
• Confit is now made in Australia and is available in gourmet shops and delis in cryovac packs.
cooking time 4-5 hours • serves 4-6

Lamb with white beans

One of the most popular dishes served at the local village feasts (or repas) in our region is lamb with white beans – in fact it is popular all over rural France. The local lamb has a totally different flavour from Australian or New Zealand lamb because the sheep graze in fields of grasses mixed with wild herbs, and it is absolutely delicious. Believe it or not, legs of frozen NZ lamb are cheaper in the French supermarkets!

2 cloves of garlic, peeled and sliced
1 leg of lamb, trimmed of excess fat
1 tablespoon unsalted butter
salt and pepper
2 tablespoons olive oil
1 onion, peeled and chopped
2 tomatoes, peeled and chopped
2 x 400g tins of white beans (haricot blanc)

Insert slices of garlic into the leg of lamb near the bone at either end – using a small sharp knife to make the incisions. Rub the lamb with butter and season with salt and pepper. Pour 1 tablespoon of the olive oil into a baking dish, add the lamb and cook in a preheated (180°) oven for 1¼ hours – slightly longer if it is a large leg. Check with a skewer – pink meat juices should still be flowing. While the lamb is cooking, in a saucepan melt the remaining olive oil and gently sauté the onion until soft and translucent. Add the tomatoes and cook slowly until they become a purée. Add the drained beans and mix together for another 5-10 minutes adding any meat juices that have drained from the lamb and seasoning with salt and pepper. The lamb should have been allowed to rest for 20 minutes. Serve on a platter surrounded by the beans.

• In France they also cook lardons (small squares of fatty bacon) with the beans. It imparts a lovely, smoky flavour but is rather fattening. After my first few long stays in France I decided to avoid lardons completely!

cooking time 1¼ hours • serves 4-6

Rabbit and prunes

In France rabbits are sold in the supermarket, either whole (with the heads still attached) or cut into handy pieces that makes preparing them much easier. They are farm-raised and very fleshy, but only require a little cooking or the meat will become tough. Cooking them with prunes – a local speciality from nearby Agen – is the perfect combination of textures and flavours.

15 prunes, stone removed

⅓ cup brandy or Armagnac

2 tablespoons olive oil

3 rashers bacon, rind removed, chopped

1 large rabbit, cut into pieces

10 small pickling onions (or 2 medium onions, peeled and chopped)

1 tablespoon plain flour

50ml good chicken stock

½ cup dry red wine

salt and pepper

sprig of fresh thyme or ¼ teaspoon dried thyme

The prunes should be soaked overnight in the brandy, until they become plump. In an enamel ovenproof casserole (with a lid) heat the olive oil and sauté the bacon pieces until they turn brown. Lift and set aside. In the same pan brown the rabbit pieces, three or four at a time so as not to overcrowd the pan. Lift and set aside. Now sauté the onions in the fat, adding a little more oil if necessary (the rabbit has very little fat and if the bacon is lean you will be running out of fat). Lastly brown the flour in the remaining fat, stirring until it is well absorbed and starts to colour. Return the bacon and rabbit with juices to the pot then pour over the stock (it is better if the stock is hot because it comes back to the boil rapidly) and red wine. Season with salt and pepper and add the thyme then cover with the lid and put the pot in a preheated (180°) oven for 25-30 minutes. Lift the lid and add the prunes along with the liquid, stirring to incorporate. Return to the oven for a further 15 minutes. Serve with buttery mashed potatoes and steamed green beans tossed in butter and garlic.

cooking time 50 minutes • serves 4-6

Blood sausages

Blood sausage and apple (Boudin Noir)

I have never enjoyed 'black pudding' as it was called when I was a child, but this version of the sausage made from pigs' blood and cooked with tart green apples is totally delicious.

2 tablespoons unsalted butter

4 tart green apples, peeled, cored and sliced

1kg blood sausage, cut into bite-sized pieces

1 tablespoon brandy

salt and pepper

Melt the butter in a heavy-based frying pan and sauté the apple pieces until they start to soften. Lift and set aside. If necessary add a dab more butter and heat until it bubbles. Add the pieces of blood sausage – not all at once – and brown on all sides, returning the sausage and the apple to the pan at the end to make sure they are all hot. Lift onto a hot serving platter and add the brandy to the pan juices, mixing with a wooden spoon. Pour over the sausage and apple, season with salt and pepper and serve immediately.

cooking time 20-25 minutes • serves 4

Cheese course

No French meal is complete without a cheese course. This is always brought to the table after the main course (plat) and before the dessert. Although we are inclined to think of cheese as high in fat and therefore bad for our cholesterol, in fact the enzymes in the cheese are a terrific aid for digestion, breaking down the fat from the rest of the meal. Eating cheese at every meal is one of the theories about why French women don't get fat.

The secret is only to eat a little cheese – not a great hearty slab. When I first started cooking for friends in France I went mad with the cheeses – buying six or more different varieties to create an impressive (and expensive) platter. Most of it remained uneaten because, simply, after the soup, entrée and plat nobody could manage vast quantities of cheese (especially if anticipating a dessert). So now I simply choose two good varieties – either a Brie or Camembert and a hard cheese like Cantal; or a soft goat cheese (or Cabécou) and a blue cheese such as Roquefort. Most of these cheese are now available in Australia and we also have many excellent cheeses of our own. My advice would be to buy the best cheese available (you can always ask for a taste at the counter) and only buy one or two varieties and in small quantities.

Red wine is always served with the cheese course as it really helps to bring out the flavour. Crusty bread is also served, but I notice that my French female friends just pop a sliver of cheese into the mouths and avoid any more bread – the prevailing wisdom is that the bread is more fattening than any other part of the meal.

Plum paste

A paste – plum or quince or apple and plum – is often served with the cheese course although fresh figs are a more simple solution. However, if you have a glut of plums (as I do at the farm) this is an excellent way of making the most of the harvest.

1kg plums, slightly under ripe
1 cup water
caster sugar
2 tablespoons lemon juice

Using slightly under-ripe plums gives them a higher pectin level, which helps the paste to set. In a heavy-based saucepan cover the plums with water and simmer until they completely soften. Strain them to remove the skin and seeds, pushing the pulp through the sieve. Weigh the plum pulp and add an equal quantity of sugar, bring back to the boil and stir to dissolve. Add the lemon juice. Keep this on a brisk simmer for 30 minutes, stirring occasionally to prevent sticking. Test for setting as you would for jam – put ¼ teaspoon on a cool saucer. If it forms a skin and is no longer runny it is ready. If not, keep cooking until it reaches this stage. Pour into a shallow loaf tin lined with baking paper and refrigerate. Cut into squares and store in an airtight container in the fridge – it should last several months.
cooking time variable

Red wine
always with
the cheese.

Strawberries in red wine

This is a simple dessert and a great way to make large strawberries more succulent. In France strawberries can only be bought in the markets in late spring/early summer and are so sweet and flavoursome that they are best eaten unadulterated – however I still sometimes dress them up in this fashion.

2 punnets fresh strawberries, hulled but not washed
½ cup caster sugar
2 cups good red wine

If the strawberries are large then cut them into halves or quarters. Sprinkle with sugar and allow this to soften for 30 minutes. Now cover with wine and allow to steep for at least 2 hours at room temperature before serving with good vanilla ice cream or creme fraiche.
serves 4-6

Dessert

No meal is complete without a little something sweet to finish. In this region the last course is often based on seasonal fruit and isn't overly sugary or smothered in cream. The boulangerie always has a marvellous selection of tarts and pastries if you aren't in the mood for cooking.

Pears Armandine

My mother regularly cooked this dessert from her *Flavour of France* cookbook and I have, in turn, cooked it for my French friends. Although from Alsace, it is well appreciated in the southwest.

¼ cup slivered almonds, lightly toasted
1 cup water
½ cup caster sugar
4 firm fresh pears, peeled and halved
1 punnet strawberries, hulled and sliced
whipped cream for serving

Toast the almonds in a dry, non-stick frying pan until lightly brown. Allow to cool. Make a sugar syrup by simmering the sugar and water together in a shallow saucepan until the sugar has dissolved. Poach the pears in this liquid for 5-8 minutes. Arrange the cooked pears on a platter, round side up, with several almonds inserted into each one. Reduce the poaching syrup by a half then add the strawberries, simmering until it reduces yet again into a syrup. Force this through a sieve and pour the sauce over the pears. Refrigerate for 1 hour. Serve with whipped cream.
cooking time 30 minutes • serves 4

Crème brûlée

This is a rich custard desert with a crunchy toffee topping that is probably one of the most popular desserts in all of France. Although it is rich, because each serving is small it is a delightful way to end even a large meal.

8 egg yolks
⅓ cup granulated white sugar
2 cups heavy cream
1 teaspoon pure vanilla extract
¼ cup granulated white sugar
   (for the caramelised tops)

Preheat oven to 170°. Whisk the egg yolks and sugar until the sugar has dissolved and the mixture is thick and pale yellow. Add the cream and vanilla, and continue to whisk until well combined. Strain through a sieve to remove any foam or bubbles. Pour the custard into 6 crème brûlée dishes or shallow ovenproof ramekins. Place in a water bath (large baking dish filled with 10-15 cm of warm water) and bake until set around the edges, but still loose in the centre, about 45 minutes. Remove cups from water bath and chill for at least 2 hours, or up to 2 days. When ready to serve, sprinkle about 2 teaspoons of sugar over each custard. For best results, use a small, hand-held blow-torch to melt sugar. If you don't have a blow-torch, place under a hot grill until the sugar melts.
cooking 45 minutes • serves 6

Spicy lamb and lentil soup (recipe p173)

The farm

Bathurst

Yetholme

Katoomba

BLUE
MOUNTAINS
NATIONAL
PARK

SYDNEY-

After six months of

tranquillity in rural France I returned to the Leura house. I was shocked by the fast pace of life in the mountains. When we first moved there with our young family in the Seventies it had been a sleepy, semi-rural community. However over two decades it had became a frantic tourist destination with the local shopping street transformed into smart cafes, trendy restaurants and expensive emporiums.

Our daughter Miriam and her family (husband Rick and three little boys) decided to move from Katoomba to the country town of Bathurst on the other side of the mountains. This motivated David and I to think about leaving our home of 26 years and moving further west to be near them.

We looked at a few farms on the outskirts of Bathurst, but only half-heartedly. Then one of the agents took us to see a newly-listed property and it was exactly what I had always imagined. A rambling old house surrounded by mature trees in a gentle rural landscape. I felt I had finally come home.

Initially, David was resistant to the idea of moving – in our 31 years together we had only lived in two houses. But I was convinced the time was right to escape from my high maintenance Leura garden and to embrace a more natural landscape. The property we chose is part of the village of Yetholme, which is 1,300 metres above sea level and probably one of the chilliest regions of NSW. I have always loved a cold climate – the appeal of open fires and cooking meals on a wood stove.

The kitchen has three alternative methods of cooking. There is a large electric stove with a spacious oven; a gas cook top with wok burner; plus the old wood-burning stove, which has an oven and a warming oven plus lots of simmering space on top.

When the whole family sits down to lunch there are eighteen, including eight grandchildren. It's a lot of work but more importantly a tremendous amount of fun.

The farmhouse is spacious and can accommodate the entire tribe, with children sleeping on inflatable beds in sleeping bags and one or two on sofas. It snows several times in winter and then in spring the garden comes alive with blossom followed by bulbs and then roses.

Early in the morning David lets the geese out to graze the paddocks and garden. There is space and freedom for the children to explore a natural environment that is adventurous and yet safe for them.

The ornamental cherry
trees continue to flower
prolifically in spite of
the drought; these days
I seldom water the
garden except to keep
the vegetable patch
alive and growing.

The farmhouse has a comparatively small kitchen, although it appears much larger because a wall has been removed between the kitchen and old laundry, which once would have housed the copper for boiling water to wash clothes and to cook the Christmas pudding wrapped in calico. The back of the house, adjacent to the laundry is the original maid's quarters consisting of a small bedroom and pretty sitting room with a fireplace and decorative window seat. This also has been opened out into one large room that we use as our 'family' living area. It's very comfortable indeed.

Long time residents of the district tell us that the kitchen originally had a large Scottish Aga wood stove that would have kept half the house warm in winter as well as heating the water for showers and baths. Sadly this was removed in the 1970s and replaced with a more modern wood-burning stove that is not very efficient or easy to cook on – unlike my good old reliable Rayburn. But I struggle on with it, and have bought a second hand Aga that sits in the shed waiting for us to have the time, energy and resources to get it installed.

For me, one of the main attractions of the house was the large walk-in pantry with most of the original shelving intact. There is also a servery from the pantry into a walkway that leads to the dining room. I can visualise meals being passed from the kitchen stove through the servery and then to the dining room with its open fire flickering in the background.

Amazingly, our furniture fitted into the old farmhouse perfectly. It was as though the long table, designed for our kitchen in Leura, had been made for the dining room at Yetholme. Even my mother's old sofas dating from the 1940s (which have been reupholstered several times) fitted perfectly into the small formal sitting room. Friends who came to stay commented that the atmosphere was very much the same – the fuel stove warming the kitchen, the open fires, the comfortable furniture and, of course, meals at the long table.

It was as though the long table had been made for the dining room at Yetholme.

I try not to look when they climb too high.

Caius at the kitchen door

Hamish and Sam

Caius and Ella

Gus

The children scatter from one end of the house and garden to another. I am happy that they have the opportunity to develop relationships as cousins — some day it will afford them wonderful memories.

Ella

They are affectionate children and
I am given plenty of hugs and
cuddles whenever they are around.
I also laugh a lot at their antics
and when they get into mischief.

The children love to help us get organised for lunch, especially when it comes to lighting the dining room fire. Here Theo, Sam, Eamonn and Hamish get a fire going for lunch.

Initially I was against creating a time-consuming garden at the farm, feeling burnt out by years of crawling around on my hands and knees pulling up weeds. However I was keen to have poultry – chickens, ducks and geese – and of course a good vegetable and herb garden. Luckily, there were already well-established fruit trees including several heirloom apple varieties, five different plums and two peach trees which I suspect, because of their location so close to the house, may have been self sown. Regardless, they produced a terrific crop of fruit during our first summer.

Best of all was the discovery of a row of mature walnut trees in the paddock behind the house. I had never considered growing nut trees during my time in the mountains, but in the southwest of France walnuts are a traditional part of the regional diet, having provided much needed protein for the peasant farmers in days gone by. During my time in France I had learned to love walnuts as the basis of a popular aperitif (eau de noix) and to use them in cooking – for both sweet and savoury recipes. And here I was in rural Australia with three magnificent trees of my own!

As a place for children, the farm is idyllic. There are the usual hazards – a stream and a couple of dams plus various venomous snakes – but the children have the freedom to run and climb trees and play games of imagination from dawn till dusk. There are now eight grandchildren in our family – six boys and two girls. Only a year after we moved to the farm our daughter and her brood moved from Bathurst to Adelaide, however her four boys often come to stay during the school holidays and at Christmas time the entire family descends for a noisy, action-packed family reunion. I am at my happiest when the house is full of children (there are five bedrooms) and I am planning breakfast, lunch and dinner to please them.

The garden in winter. The original community hall behind the house is a great play area for children when the weather is bad. Inside it has wooden floors, a theatrical stage complete with open fireplace and, at the other end of the hall, a small kitchen.

During summer I encourage the children to stay outdoors as much as possible. I sometimes pack a picnic lunch and give them a trolley to carry it all, then send them off to the back paddock for an hour or so. I can sort of see them in the distance from the kitchen door and the dog (Luscious the labrador) goes with them, probably because she gets to feast on the leftovers.

The children love planning menus with me, and I encourage each of them to choose an evening meal they would like me to prepare, taking it in turns. What they choose often surprises me. The oldest, Eamonn, loves old-fashioned meatloaf and at 13 he is now more than capable of making it himself with a bit of supervision. Sam, number two grandson, asks for roast duck with chestnuts and Brussels sprouts which ends up being quite a costly exercise if the whole family is in attendance. Hamish, my grandson from Mudgee, loves the summer months because he can pick sweet corn from the garden, plus tomatoes of course. The others love just about anything, and I give them cookbooks to help them choose their special dinner. It gives such a focus to the day and it's refreshing to see them so involved and enthusiastic.

I also encourage them to help as much as possible. They all like peeling vegetables and they take turns to lay the table – setting out the candles, the wine glasses and the cloth table napkins – and they love helping to make dessert. Again they tend to choose

The dining room set for
lunch. On cold days we light
the open fire and the room
heats up very quickly,
especially when crowded with
people and platters of hot
food. At night the heavy
curtains are drawn to
maintain the warmth.

Our flock of geese was inherited from a neighbour and the size of the flock varies according to the success of various predators. In spite of a fox-proof cage where they are locked at night we still seem to lose a few, especially in late winter which is mating and egg-laying time.

Old sheds of corrugated iron with paint peeling from timber doors.

> In a way this farm is the place I always dreamed about for my own children when they were growing up, with open space and freedom.

old-fashioned favourites – custards, stewed fruits, pavlova, pancakes and fruit pies. The quantity of food they get through is alarming – David does most of the shopping and claims he needs a truck to bring home supplies when the children are in residence.

In France children are trained from an early age to sit at a meal table with their family, often for more than an hour at a time. This is the most fantastic way of socialising them, as they learn to share the meal and to converse naturally with adults. Children here tend to be more restless and would rather eat sitting in front of a television set. Naturally I am totally opposed to this concept. So I am firm with the children about sitting through the meal and participating just as their parents did when growing up at Leura. Some of my grandchildren are easier to wrangle than others, but they are all getting better at remaining in their places for the entire meal. It helps if we have a conversation game to keep them occupied. Last school holidays I suggested that each child relate a family story during the meal – just some little memory or anecdote from the past that had made them laugh. They had the whole day to come up with their story ideas and I often heard them discussing and planning when they were playing outside. Some of the stories were hilarious. This not only helps them to develop memory and language skills but provides great entertainment for all of us.

We have quite a large flock of geese, but we have killed and eaten very few because of the work involved. Unlike chickens, which are comparatively easy to pluck and dress, geese can take hours to prepare because they have three layers of feathers including the fine white 'down' feathers that protect their entire body from the cold. One Christmas my son-in-law killed a young goose and it took my daughter Miriam more than two hours to pluck it. I gathered all the down feathers into an old pillowslip and hung them in one of the sheds

I am delighted that
my grandchildren
enjoy being here so
much, climbing trees
and exploring the
back paddocks.

The dog, Luscious the Labrador, follows the boys wherever they roam. From the kitchen door I can hear the sound of their laughter and yelps of delight.

The house is more comfortable than stylish and I have deliberately left the old and worn carpet so that I can feel relaxed when the place is full of children and pets. There is no fuss!

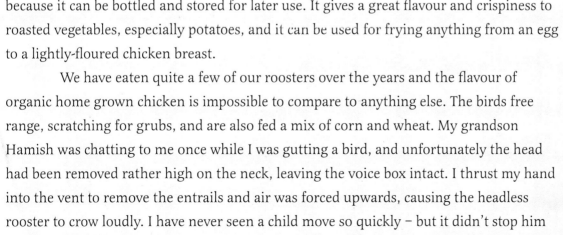

I'm inclined to let plants grow rampantly — I never was a stickler for pruning — and prefer the garden being wild rather than neat and tamed.

Weedy grass and trees makes for a low maintenance garden in most areas. Despite the lack of rain most of the trees are thriving.

to dry out. On Christmas morning the lawn was covered with white feathers – it looked like snow – and we realised the dog had managed to jump up and pull the pillowslip down and then shaken it all around the garden. To her the feathers must have smelt wonderful!

The flesh of a young goose is tender and delicious if roasted slowly, but the older geese taste like rubber unless cooked with great care. They need to be roasted twice – once at a very low heat to extract as much of the fat as possible and the second time to make the skin crisp. For my taste, the fat from the goose is the most worthwhile portion, because it can be bottled and stored for later use. It gives a great flavour and crispiness to roasted vegetables, especially potatoes, and it can be used for frying anything from an egg to a lightly-floured chicken breast.

We have eaten quite a few of our roosters over the years and the flavour of organic home grown chicken is impossible to compare to anything else. The birds free range, scratching for grubs, and are also fed a mix of corn and wheat. My grandson Hamish was chatting to me once while I was gutting a bird, and unfortunately the head had been removed rather high on the neck, leaving the voice box intact. I thrust my hand into the vent to remove the entrails and air was forced upwards, causing the headless rooster to crow loudly. I have never seen a child move so quickly – but it didn't stop him from eating the chicken dinner that evening. He did, however, ask 'is it really dead now?'

The farm

We have well defined roles,
although everyone lends a hand
and very few orders are issued.
I prepare and cook the meals helped
by my daughter and daughters-in-
law; the boys set the table,
assisted by the children; David
carves and does all the cleaning
up afterwards. It works.

Over time our grandchildren have learned that sitting at the table with adults is fun. They get lots of good food and are encouraged to participate in the conversation, often with hilarious results.

I am comfort... with myself wh... the house is full of childr...

I struggled with the vegetable garden initially. It was located on the site of a pre-existing vegetable garden that had great soil but was a long way from the nearest tap, making watering rather labour intensive. Then we created a much smaller garden on the site of the old poultry enclosure, knowing that the soil was enriched with decades of manure. This garden has been much easier to maintain because it is fenced (from rabbits) with a rosemary hedge that helps to keep the weeds down. The other garden was more open and exposed so that every imaginable paddock weed took root.

During summer I grow potatoes, tomatoes (six varieties), beans, salad greens, carrots, beetroot, corn, all my herbs and anything else the family fancies. In winter it's cauliflower, broccoli, Brussels sprouts, broad beans, cabbage and garlic. I have also planted currants, raspberries, gooseberries and asparagus but most of them, along with the strawberries, were lost in last summer's drought. Our water supply from the spring dried up – it had been providing water for this house and garden for almost a hundred years. Since then we have been using a rainwater tank and trucking in additional water by tanker. Which is why I simply had to allow some areas of the garden to go. Time will tell what bounces back next spring after good winter rains.

In spite of this situation I have had a couple of bumper summer crops, with the busiest time of year being autumn when the tomatoes and potatoes are ready for harvesting. The oven is kept going for hours at a time processing the tomatoes for the freezer. I fill shallow baking dishes with the ripest tomatoes, roughly chopped and combined with carrots, onion, garlic and various herbs tossed in good olive oil. This is roasted until caramelised then put through a blender to make a rich tomato pulp that is frozen in individual plastic containers. The last two seasons have been good enough to keep us supplied with this sauce until the following year's crop is ready to harvest. I use it on pasta or add it to stews.

Over the years I have accumulate
nothing is so important that it
The people in our lives are much

I am sure that our children and grandchildren have attachments to various bits and pieces around the house and I must make sure they end up with their favourites…familiar objects are the most treasured.

a lot of beautiful objects, but
s broken I would be upset.
ore valuable …

I love the house with
its tall chimneys and deep verandahs.
It will be a sad day when
we have to leave it behind,
but I guess these are realities
we all have to face.

Kitchen Closed
This chook's stuffed!

Every home has an atmosphere
that reflects the people who live
in it. Our houses have always been
colourful, crowded and a little
shabby but very well loved.

Sid the cat

My mother's old sofas with
feather cushions that have been
recovered five times. I expect
they'll still be around in fifty years.

The potatoes are dug and allowed to dry in the sun for a few hours before being packed carefully between thick layers of newspaper in cardboard boxes kept in the darkest corner of the shed (in a rat-proof cage). They last for up to six months this way, certainly right through the winter.

The other autumn job is gathering the walnuts, which fall to the ground and must be picked up immediately. We compete with the cockatoos (a pest problem they don't encounter in France) but still manage to harvest a huge quantity. The green husks must be removed and the walnuts dried and bleached in the sun (commercially they use real bleach, so this method is much healthier). Gloves need to be worn because the husks produce an unpleasant black stain that marks skin. Sometimes I use semi-ripe walnuts to make eau de noix (walnut liquor). The first year I spent hours cleaning and pricking the green walnut husks then steeping them in large jars, covering them with brandy. The recipe required that the jars be set in the sun every day for two weeks and I religiously carried the jars out and put them on a small table in the garden. Luscious, unfortunately, became curious and one day jumped up to look (suspecting there could be food left lying around) knocking the three jars to the ground, smashing them. I don't know if she licked up the residue!

Another seasonal task is processing the apples and plums, again in vast quantities. The apples are peeled, stewed and bottled while the plums are either made into jam or various sauces, or the juice is extracted to make a wonderfully rich plum jelly. I have invested in a splendid pot from Finland that steam extracts the juice from any type of fruit, so in summer I also make apple juice, which the children just love. It is cloudy and has virtually no sugar but the most intense apple flavour.

To really make the most of the land available to us at the farm I would need to live here all year round and have no other work or commitments (no writing books, no trips to France, no trekking in the Himalayas). Growing food for the table is tremendous fun and deeply satisfying, but to do it properly is very time consuming. However, I consider myself to be very fortunate indeed even to produce at least a percentage of what we eat and to have the pleasure of harvesting it and cooking it for the family.

Chicken laksa

Soups

Homemade soup remains our preferred fast and easy meal. Although these days we enjoy spicy Asian soups as much, if not more, than our traditional family favourites. At this altitude even the summers are often cold at night, and that's when soup really comes into its own.

Favourite recipes

Spicy lamb and lentil soup

This is a hearty winter soup that is rich and flavoursome. Add extra chilli if you like your soup hot and spicy.

2 litres lamb stock
diced meat from 2 lamb shanks (used to make stock)
1-2 tablespoons olive oil
1 onion, peeled and diced
2 medium carrots, peeled and sliced
2 parsnips, peeled and sliced
2 medium potatoes, peeled and chopped
2 stems of celery, washed and chopped
½ red capsicum, chopped
1 medium tomato, peeled and chopped
500g brown lentils
salt and pepper
½ teaspoon hot paprika
½-1 teaspoon chilli paste (depending on taste)
finely chopped parsley

Make the stock the day before by simmering 2 lamb shanks in 3 litres of water, skimming any froth, for 1 hour. If you want you can throw in half an onion, a small carrot, and some celery and peppercorns to improve the flavour (I usually do this when making stock). Lift the shanks and allow them to cool, and then remove the meat and chop. Strain the stock and refrigerate overnight.

In a large soup pot heat the oil and fry the onion until soft and translucent. Add the carrots, parsnips, potatoes, celery, capsicum and tomato, and continue to cook for a few minutes to infuse the flavours. Season with salt and pepper, paprika and chilli paste. Add the lamb stock and bring to the boil, then turn down to a simmer. Wash and drain the lentils. Add these to the soup along with the chopped meat. Simmer for 45 minutes until vegetables and lentils are well cooked. Add more water if it has become too thick. Garnish with chopped parsley when serving.

• Most soups, and stews, curries and casseroles as well, are better the day after they have been cooked. It's difficult to be organised in advance, but if possible work a day ahead. You will enjoy soups that have a much more mature flavour.

cooking time 1½-2 hours • serves 4-6

Chicken laksa

This is my own version of the classic Malaysian soup that is hearty enough to serve as a meal on its own.

1.5-2 litres chicken stock
1 tablespoon peanut oil
1 bunch shallots, chopped
15-20 snow peas, stems removed
1 small bunch bok choy, rinsed and chopped
1-2 tablespoons good quality laksa paste
1 packet bean sprouts, rinsed and drained
2 cooked chicken breasts, torn into small pieces
1 tin light coconut milk
about 250g vermicelli noodles
1 small bunch bok choy, rinsed and chopped
extra chilli (optional)
½ bunch coriander, torn
stock
1.5-2 litres water
1 free range or corn fed chicken
10 cm section of ginger, peeled and chopped
3 garlic cloves, peeled
small green chilli, halved
2 or 3 celery tops
½ teaspoon salt

Make the stock the day before. Put the water in a large soup pot and add the other ingredients. Bring to the boil then turn down to simmer for 1¼ hours until the chicken is well cooked. Lift the chicken and allow to cool. Strain the stock through a fine sieve and refrigerate overnight. Remove the skin from the chicken and separate the meat from the bones. Not all the meat will be needed for the laksa and I keep the rest to mix with mayonnaise for sandwiches.

Use a wok to make the laksa. Skim the fat from the chicken stock and bring it to simmering point in a large saucepan. Heat the oil in the wok and lightly stir-fry the shallots, snow peas and bok choy – just for a few minutes. Add the laksa paste and fry it off – then add the bean sprouts and pieces of chicken. Now add the hot stock and coconut milk and turn the heat down. In the saucepan used for the stock boil some water and add the noodles (use more if you like). They only take a couple of minutes to soften. Strain the noodles and put them into large Asian bowls. Ladle the hot laksa over the top and add extra chilli if desired. Garnish with torn leaves of coriander.

cooking time 1½ hours • serves 6

Broad bean salad with mint

Summer lunches

Although we have maintained Sunday lunch as a hot meal, on Saturdays when I garden from early morning, we like to stop for some lunch – something more than just a sandwich – with a glass of chilled wine (I drink the wine, David usually sticks to water).

Broad bean salad with mint

We grow broad beans at the farm. My daughter-in-law Simone, whose family is from Malta, loves them more than any other vegetable, so I guess they must have childhood associations.

2kg young broad beans in their pods
3 sprigs fresh mint
6-8 slices prosciutto
1 small cos lettuce heart
½ cup good olive oil
2 tablespoons red wine vinegar
1 teaspoon Dijon mustard
salt and pepper

Remove the pods from the broad beans and cook them in boiling water for 30 seconds. Peel the second layer of skin, revealing the small, pale green fava beans in the centre. Finely slice the leaves of the mint and bang the stems with a meat mallet a few times to bring out the flavour. Put the mint leaves and stems into a pot of boiling water and add the young tender beans, cooking for 3 minutes. Strain and remove the stems. Cut the prosciutto into very fine strips. Wash and tear the lettuce into small pieces. Mix together the prosciutto, beans and lettuce. Make a dressing by whisking together the olive oil, vinegar and mustard. Season with salt and pepper. Toss the dressing into the salad and serve immediately.
cooking time 3-4 minutes • serves 4

Pear and Roquefort salad

4 ripe pears, peeled, cored and sliced
1 tablespoon lemon juice
6 tablespoons walnut oil
1 tablespoon white wine vinegar
1 teaspoon grain mustard
salt and pepper
2 cups rocket leaves, washed
1 cup walnut pieces
75g Roquefort cheese, crumbled

Drizzle the pear slices with lemon juice to prevent them from turning brown. Make a dressing by putting the walnut oil, vinegar, mustard and salt into a jar and shaking until well combined.
In the base of a bowl put the torn rocket, followed by the pears and walnuts and lastly the crumbled Roquefort. Drizzle the dressing over the salad and finish with freshly ground black pepper.
serves 4-6

Seafood pilaf

I love meals that are cooked all in one pot because of the wonderful amalgamation of flavours. This one is a cross between paella and a pilaf.

2 tablespoons olive oil
1 onion, peeled and chopped
2 cloves garlic, peeled and sliced
2 small carrots, peeled and sliced thinly
2 tomatoes, peeled and chopped
½ red capsicum, diced
1 small red chilli, finely chopped
1½ cups long grain rice
6 threads of saffron
¼ cup boiling water
3 cups hot fish stock
salt and pepper
500g boneless salmon
500g boneless white fish
300g peeled green prawns
1 cup frozen peas
1 tablespoon finely chopped parsley

In a wide flat-bottom pan (with a lid) heat the olive oil and sauté the onion until soft and translucent. Add the garlic for a few minutes, stirring with a wooden spoon. Now add the carrots, tomatoes, capsicum and chilli and cook for 10 minutes on low heat, stirring to help the flavours to amalgamate. Now add the rice and stir well so that the grains are well coated. Pour the boiling water over the saffron threads and allow to steep for 10 minutes. Pour this over the vegetables – it should bubble furiously – then pour on the hot fish stock and stir well so that the ingredients are fully covered by the liquid. Add salt and freshly ground black pepper. Cover and put on the lowest heat for 20-25 minutes. Don't stir because the rice will cook by absorbing the liquid. Check that the rice is cooked – if not quite done add a couple of tablespoons of hot water and replace the lid for 5 minutes more. Now add the chopped fish, prawns and peas. Incorporate lightly into hot rice and vegetables with a fork and replace the lid for 5-6 minutes. Sprinkle with finely chopped parsley. Serve with sourdough bread and green salad.
cooking time 55 minutes • serves 4

Potato salad

1kg waxy potatoes, peeled
300ml Greek yoghurt (or crème fraîche)
150ml mayonnaise
1 onion, peeled and chopped very finely
1 small bunch chives, chopped finely
2 tablespoon Dijon mustard
1 teaspoon raw sugar
salt and pepper

Boil potatoes whole and check to make sure they are cooked but not overcooked (they should still be firm). Mix all the other ingredients together and then add the sliced potatoes while still warm – they will absorb the dressing better this way. Allow to cool and serve at room temperature.
cooking time 20 minutes • serves 4-6

Asian steamed fish

Although we live well away from the ocean, we try and eat fish at least once a week and this is a favourite method.

1-1.5kg boneless white fish fillets
1 teaspoon Asian cooking oil
15 cm stem of ginger, peeled and grated
1 bunch of shallots, washed and chopped
4 cloves of garlic, peeled and crushed
1 small red chilli, chopped finely
1 teaspoon crushed lemon grass
2 tablespoons soy sauce

Use the widest aluminium foil and take off a section that is 45-60 cm in length. In a bowl put all the ingredients and mix together by hand so that the fish pieces are thoroughly coated. Allow to marinate for 30 minutes, then put onto the foil, making sure the fillets of fish are laying flat – you can make two layers if necessary. Seal the foil tightly and place in a preheated oven (180°) and cook for 30 minutes. Serve with rice.
cooking time 30 minutes • serves 4

Seafood pilaf

San choy bao (lettuce cups)

It's the combination of the fragrant pork mince and the crisp lettuce leaves that's so delicious.

2 tablespoons san choy boa sauce

1 small onion, finely chopped

500g pork mince

230g tin bamboo shoots, drained and chopped finely

2 tablespoons Asian cooking oil

8 large iceburg lettuce leaves, washed and trimmed
   to a cup shape

In a wok heat the oil and stir-fry the onion until well done. Add the pork mince and continue to cook until brown and finely crumbled. Add the chopped bamboo shoots and the sauce and stir to incorporate. Turn down to low heat and cook for a further 10 minutes. Serve the hot mince in a bowl and the lettuce cups on a platter. People can help themselves, scooping the mince into the lettuce and folding it over into a parcel. Eat with your fingers.

cooking time 15-20 minutes • serves 4

Spatchcock with rice and olives

Some supermarkets sell plump spatchcock (size 5) that are quite meaty and will remain moist if not overcooked. This is an 'all in one pot' meal where the rice soaks up all the delicious flavours.

2 spatchcocks
1 tablespoon Middle Eastern herb rub
2 tablespoons olive oil
1 onion, peeled and chopped
2 cloves garlic, peeled and crushed
2 carrots, peeled and sliced thinly
2 tomatoes, peeled and chopped
20 pitted Kalamata olives
1 cup rice
½ cup white wine
1½ cups boiling water
salt and pepper
finely chopped parsley for serving

Rub the herbs into the halved spatchcocks and allow to sit for 30 minutes to absorb some of the flavours. Heat the oil in a heavy-based, wide pan (with a lid) and brown the spatchcocks on both sides. Remove and set aside. Add a little more oil if necessary and sauté the onions until soft and translucent. Add the garlic and cook for 2 minutes, then the carrots, tomatoes and olives. Cook on low heat for 10 minutes, stirring with a wooden spoon from time to time. Add the rice and coat it thoroughly with the other ingredients then splash on the wine – it will bubble – followed by 1 cup of boiling water. Stir well, season with salt and pepper and cover the pan to get the rice cooking for about 10 minutes. Then return the spatchcocks to the pan, cut side down. I gently push them into the rice so they almost touch the base of the pan. Replace the lid and cook for another 20-25 minutes. Check to make sure the rice is cooked – if still a bit hard in the middle add some more boiling water and cook for a few minutes longer. Garnish with chopped parsley and serve immediately.
• I sometimes throw a small tin of anchovies in at the last minute – the ones that are wrapped around a caper. They add piquancy.

cooking time 50 minutes • serves 2

Spatchcock with rice and olives

Nonna's red peppers

My daughter-in-law Lynne is descended from a Sicilian family and her gorgeous grandmother, Nonna, brings this to me every time she visits the farm. Her grandfather, Nonno, makes his own wine and still grows most of their vegetables.

6 red capsicums
olive oil
½ teaspoon sea salt

Put the grill on high (or use the barbecue, also on high). Cut the capsicums into quarters, removing the seeds, and brush with olive oil. Place under the grill in batches and keep an eye on them – the idea is for the skin to turn black and blister. As each batch is done place inside a plastic bag and close the top – this will cause the capsicum to sweat. After half an hour take the pieces out and peel off the skin – it should come easily. I sometimes rinse them under cold water and lay out on a paper towel to dry. Cut into thin slices and put in a bowl, covering with a good quality olive oil and crushed salt. Cover the bowl and allow to steep overnight before serving.

cooking time 20 minutes • serves 4-6

Favourite recipes

Main meals

A lot of the meals I make these days are in one pot – either casseroles and stews or rice dishes cooked on top of the stove in a wide and shallow pan with a lid. The flavours infuse wonderfully when food is cooked this way and it's so much easier than cooking meat and vegetables separately in four or five different pots.

Szechwan chicken

1 tablespoon dark soy sauce
2 teaspoons Chinese rice vinegar
½ teaspoon five spice powder
5 cm stem ginger, peeled and sliced
6-8 cloves garlic, peeled and sliced
500g chicken thigh fillets, diced
3 tablespoons vegetable oil
1 small white onion, peeled and diced finely
1 red capsicum, diced
1½ tablespoons Szechuan peppercorns
chilli bean paste (to taste)
6 shallots, sliced

Make a marinade of the soy sauce, vinegar, five spice powder, half the ginger and half the garlic. Mix the chicken pieces into this marinade, coating them thoroughly, and cover. Refrigerate overnight.
Drain the marinade from the chicken and spices and reserve both. In a large wok heat about 2 tablespoons of oil on high and stir-fry the chicken, in two batches, until cooked – 5-7 minutes per batch. Drain the wok – leaving about 1 tablespoon of oil and stir-fry the onion for a minute, then add the capsicum and cook for another minute. Add the peppercorns, chilli bean paste and shallots, tossing them with the other ingredients. Add the remaining ginger and garlic and continue to cook on high. After a minute add the marinade and the chicken. Cook for a further 2 minutes to heat through and serve with steamed rice.
cooking time 20-25 minutes • serves 4

French lamb stew

This is a tasty alternative to the traditional Irish stew, the main difference being that the meat is braised and not boiled and, being French, wine is also an important ingredient. In my mother's *Flavour of France* it is called Navarin de Mouton.

2 tablespoons olive oil
2 onions, peeled and diced
2 cloves garlic, peeled and crushed
1-1.5kg lean lamb stewing chops, fat removed
1 tablespoon plain flour
salt and pepper
1 cup white wine
2 cups water
3-4 carrots, peeled and sliced
3-4 parsnips, peeled and sliced
4 large potatoes, peeled and quartered
1½ cup frozen peas
1 tablespoon parsley, finely chopped

In a heavy-based cooking pot with a lid heat the oil and sauté the onion until soft and translucent. Add the garlic for 2 minutes, stirring to prevent it from burning, then lift the onion and garlic and reserve. Add more oil to the pan if necessary. Cut the lamb into large chunks. In a plastic bag toss the meat in the flour, salt and pepper then brown in the oil in three batches – shaking off the excess flour as you go. Throw the wine onto the browned meat – it should bubble furiously, then add the water and cover, turning the heat to low. After 30 minutes add the carrots and parsnips and stir, replacing the lid. Cook for another 30 minutes then add the potato chunks – if they cook too long they will crumble and they should only need about 25 minutes. Push the potatoes into the stew with a wooden spoon to make sure they are well covered. Five minutes before serving add the peas and sprinkle the chopped parsley on top just before bringing the stew – in the pot – to the table. Some fresh bread and a green salad is all you will need to make a delicious meal.
cooking time 1½ hours • served 4-6

French lamb stew

David's lamb shanks

David's lamb shanks

David's favourite meat is lamb and his favourite cut of lamb is the shank. This slow-cooked stew is best cooked the day before and reheated gently.

3 tablespoons olive oil
4-6 large lamb shanks, Frenched
1 teaspoon plain flour
salt and pepper
1 onion, peeled and chopped
2 cloves garlic, peeled and crushed
2 carrots, peeled and sliced
2 parsnips, peeled and sliced
2 tomatoes, peeled and diced
½ cup red wine
1½ cups water

In a heavy-based cooking pot with a lid heat the oil. Lightly dust the lamb shanks with flour, salt and pepper and brown them, two at a time, in the oil. Set aside. Add a little more oil to the pan and sauté the onion until soft and translucent, then add the garlic and cook for another minute, stirring with a wooden spoon. Add the carrots, parsnips and tomatoes and allow to cook for 5-10 minutes until the flavours have amalgamated. Return the shanks to the pot, add the wine and water and turn the heat down to very low. Cover the pot and allow the stew to simmer slowly for an hour at least – the meat should be almost falling from the bone. Serve with mashed potato, rice or buttered noodles.

cooking time 1¼ hours • serves 4

Rack of lamb with Italian vegetables

My daughter-in-law Lynne taught me how to roast vegetables Italian-style.

2 onions, peeled and quartered
4 small zucchinis, top and tailed, halved and cut into lengths
3 sticks of celery, cut into lengths
4 carrots, peeled, halved and cut into lengths
2 large potatoes, peeled and cut into wedges
1 red capsicum, seeded and cut into wide strips
2-3 tablespoons olive oil
½ teaspoon Italian mixed herbs
salt and pepper
2 racks of lamb (3 chops per person)

Preheat the oven to 190°. In a baking dish place the prepared vegetables and pour over the olive oil and sprinkle with the herbs, salt and pepper. Coat the vegetables in the oil, tossing them by hand. Put in the oven and start cooking. In a separate pan place the lamb racks, drizzled with oil and seasoned with salt and pepper. These should take no longer than 35 minutes to cook. I tend to swap the two baking dishes from one shelf to another so they both get a turn at the top of the oven to brown. The vegetables should be slightly caramelised and the lamb still pink on the inside. Serve with a green salad.

cooking time 45-50 minutes • serves 4-6

Stuffed loin of pork

A rolled loin of pork, without the fat, is an economical and non-fatty meal. However, if you like crackling – and don't indulge too often – it's even more appealing. Especially for children.

2-3kg loin of pork
3 tablespoons olive oil
stuffing
1½ tablespoons butter
1 onion, finely chopped
2 cups soft breadcrumbs
1 green apple, peeled, cored and diced
150g dried cranberries
salt and pepper
¼ teaspoon finely chopped sage or thyme

Untie the rolled loin and open it out. Lay the stuffing down the centre and roll up again, holding it together with cooking string.

Preheat the oven to 220° and heat the oil in the baking dish. Rub salt onto the outside and plunge the pork into the hot oil (skin side down if making crackling) and cook for 10 minutes. Turn the pork roll over and turn the oven down to 180°. Cook for 1¼ to 1½ hours, basting every 15 minutes. Allow the pork to rest for 15 minutes before carving. Serve with either roasted or mashed potatoes and steamed cabbage.

To make the suffing, melt the butter in a heavy frying pan and sauté the onions until soft and translucent. Allow to cool then mix together with the breadcrumbs, apple and cranberries and season with salt, pepper and herbs.

cooking time 1½ hours • serves 4-6

We love our collection of old black and white family photographs and all branches of the family are represented on the dining room wall.

Roast goose with stuffing

The only goose worth cooking is a young goose – one weighing about 4 kg – because older birds are tough and tend to be greasy. If you can buy the goose with it's gizzards (heart and liver) this will help to make a delicious stuffing.

1 goose
½ cup chicken stock
2 tablespoons butter
salt and pepper
½ teaspoon of hot paprika
stuffing
1 onion, peeled and chopped
2 tablespoons butter
goose gizzards, chopped
1 cup rice, cooked and drained
2 tablespoons chopped parsley
2 tablespoons raisins
salt and pepper

Rinse the goose under a cold tap then dry thoroughly, inside and out. Fill with the stuffing and pour the chicken stock inside the bird before trussing it up – this helps to keep it moist. Rub the skin of the goose with butter and sprinkle with salt, pepper and paprika. Roast in a baking dish, upside down, in a moderate oven (190°) for 2 hours or more, basting regularly. It will exude a lot of fat which can be scooped out at various intervals – save this fat in a jar in the fridge for cooking at a later stage. Serve the goose with steamed red cabbage and plain peeled, boiled potatoes with butter and black pepper.
To make the stuffing, sauté the onions in the butter in a heavy-based frying pan until soft and translucent then brown the goose gizzards for about 5 minutes. Cool slightly then add the rice, parsley, raisins, salt and pepper, combining with a wooden spoon.
cooking time 2-2½ hours • serves 6

Osso Bucco with gremolata

2 medium onions, peeled and chopped
1-1.5kg of veal shin slices with the bone in
1 tablespoon plain flour
salt and pepper
2 tablespoons olive oil
3 sticks celery, chopped finely
sprig fresh rosemary
½ cup dry red wine
1 tablespoon vermouth
¾ cup water or beef stock
gremolata
1 tablespoon lemon zest
4 garlic cloves, peeled and crushed
1 tablespoon finely chopped parsley

In a heavy-based cooking pot with a lid (one that can be transferred to the oven) heat the olive oil. Trim the fat from the outside of the veal slices and lightly dust with the flour, salt and pepper. Brown the veal – 2 pieces at a time – then return all the veal to the pan and add the onion, celery and rosemary, braising gently for 3-5 minutes. Add the wine and vermouth and allow to bubble for a minute before adding the stock. Put the lid on the pot and place in a preheated oven (160°) for 1 hour, until the veal is tender. Combine the lemon zest, garlic and parsley and stir into the stew just before serving. Season with some cracked pepper and serve with rice and a mixed salad.
cooking time 1¼ hour • serves 4

Christmas lunch

Curiously, for a family who ignored Mother's Day, Father's Day, Valentine's Day and all other commercially driven 'occasions', we always made a big fuss at Christmas. The food at Christmas has remained traditional in our family – no matter how hot the summer we roast a stuffed turkey and glaze a ham – although we no longer make a boiled pudding but opt for a more cooling dessert such as wine trifle or tiramisu.

For most of my adult life I have cooked on a wood stove and this makes the task even more daunting on Christmas Day. In Leura I needed to get up at 5.30am to get the stove going so that the temperature would be high enough for the turkey to start cooking at 8.30 or 9am (depending on its size). Now I have two ovens – one electric and one wood, and tend to have them both going at once – with windows and doors wide open in the hope that cooling breezes will sweep away some of the heat from the kitchen. Flies are ALWAYS a problem in rural areas, and I have literally dozens of gauze food covers in the kitchen.

One Christmas at the farm I was cooking an enormous turkey in the large electric oven and had the wood stove going full tilt in preparation for roasting the potatoes and parsnips in some of my treasured goose fat. Momentarily distracted by the phone I allowed the oven temperature to soar and the fat caught fire, sending flames shooting into the kitchen. The entire stove had turned red and was throbbing as if about to explode. The children were evacuated to the garden along with the dogs and it took my sons and son-in-law 20 minutes to get things under control. In the meantime the fire brigade had been called and they arrived to a house full of smoke and a Christmas lunch in tatters. All was rescued. I took the turkey out of the electric oven ahead of time and it kept cooking wrapped in foil and a woollen blanket and then put the parboiled potatoes into a fresh batch of goose fat and got them crisp in no time. We ate an hour later than usual, after steadying ourselves with some champagne, and once it cooled down the wood stove completely recovered from the ordeal.

Glazed ham

The ham should be glazed the day before and stored in the fridge overnight. At Christmas time refrigerator space is always at a premium – the drinks are chilled in eskies with ice or in the old fridge in the garage. After the meal the ham should be stored in an old pillowslip (or calico bag) to keep it moist. I also keep the skin and cover the carved side of the ham with that before bagging and refrigerating it.

1 cup red wine
1 cup bourbon
1 cup brown sugar
3 tablespoons grated orange rind
1 cooked leg of ham
cloves

Combine the red wine, bourbon, sugar and orange rind to make the marinade.

Skin the ham carefully, leaving a good thick layer of fat over the surface. Score across this fat with a sharp knife in a diamond pattern and insert a clove in the centre of each diamond. Place the ham in a baking dish, cover with the marinade glaze and place in a preheated oven at 180°. Every 10 minutes baste the ham with the marinade to produce a wonderful, light brown and glossy finish to the patterned fat. Looks sensational on the Christmas table – almost a shame to carve it!
cooking time 30 minutes

One year we had cold seafood and salads on Christmas day and the children complained bitterly for weeks afterwards. It just wasn't the same for them. So I maintain the traditional fare and sometimes do the same meal in the middle of winter, when the weather is more suitable, just for the fun of it.

The Rural Fire Brigade - unexpected guests on Christmas Day.

Roast turkey,
baked potatoes,
sweet potatoes,
beans and carrots

Stuffed turkey

The turkey stuffing I always go back to is the old-fashioned bread, bacon, onion and herb recipe. I have a baking 'cradle' to hold the turkey above the roasting pan, and I cook it upside down to help keep the breast moist.

stuffing

1 loaf stale white bread (4-5 days old)
60g unsalted butter
2 large brown onions, peeled and chopped finely
5-6 rashers lean bacon, chopped
1 tablespoon grated lemon rind
fresh parsley, sage, thyme, rosemary, oregano, chopped finely
salt and cracked black pepper

Chop the crusts from the bread and process into crumbs in the food processor. Melt the butter in a heavy-based frying pan and sauté the onions until soft and translucent, adding the chopped bacon towards the end. Keep cooking until the bacon has browned. Cool slightly. Mix with the breadcrumbs, lemon rind and herbs, seasoning with salt and pepper.

Roast turkey

Try to order a fresh turkey that hasn't been frozen or 'pre-basted'. These tend to go watery in the cooking. Rinse the bird and dry thoroughly, inside and out, with an old, clean tea towel. Stuff from both ends – pack the stuffing in firmly but don't cram it into so hard that it forms a solid lump. Leftover stuffing can be wrapped in aluminium foil and heated in the oven at the last minute – you can never have TOO MUCH stuffing. Use small skewers to truss the openings. Wrap the ends of the drumsticks in old squares of cotton fabric that have been soaked overnight in olive oil, then cover this with aluminium foil to help prevent the thin ends from shrinking too much. Rub oil into the skin of the turkey and place it, upside down, in a metal cradle that will hold it above the baking dish (rub oil on the cradle too as a precaution against the skin sticking). Baste every 20 minutes using a turkey baster – it's far easier than trying to tip the heavy pan and use a spoon.

The cooking time will vary according to the size of the bird. The temperature should be set at 180°. For a 5kg turkey (stuffed) allow 3½ hours. I cook the turkey upside down for the first 2½-3 hours, and then turn it over to brown the breast for 30 minutes. I take the bird out 30 minutes before serving because it will continue to cook if turned upside down and covered with aluminium foil and two old towels – make sure to cover it well or flies will find a way inside. When the bird has been lifted the potatoes and other roasted vegetables can be put on the top shelf and the temperature turned to 210° or more to get brown and turn crunchy. While the potatoes are cooking and the turkey is resting, make the gravy in the baking dish in which the bird was cooked following the basic gravy making method (page 35). If the bird has come with giblets these are great for the gravy. Chop them finely and boil for 20 minutes in a small saucepan of water. When browning the gravy flour in the baking dish put the strained giblets in the pan and mash them with the wooden spoon. Then use the boiling liquid, along with the water from cooking the vegetables, and you will produce a rich and flavoursome sauce.

Baked potatoes

Use waxy potatoes that have been peeled, cut into large chunks and parboiled for 10-12 minutes. Make sure they have been drained and are dry before plunging into hot cooking fat. I use goose or duck fat but it can be hard to source. Buy a duck and cook it the week before Christmas, saving every skerrick of the fat that oozes from the bird during the cooking. I have jars of this precious fat in the refrigerator – my daughter Miriam calls it 'Mum's fat collection'.

Sweet potato

This vegetable goes so well with roast turkey but I avoid the American fad of topping it with toasted marshmallows. Instead I peel several large sweet potatoes and steam the chunks until well cooked, then mash them at the last moment with lots of butter, salt and freshly ground black pepper. Save the boiling water for the gravy.

Beans and carrots

Use a large quantity of young beans, topped and tailed and lightly steamed. The carrots are peeled and sliced and also steamed. If I have time I glaze the cooked carrots by melting a little butter in the cooking pot and adding a spoonful of brown sugar. The cooked carrots are tossed in this, over a low heat, before serving.

Grandma's trifle

Part of the preparation for this can be done the day before, but the trifle itself will need to be assembled on the day – several hours at least before the meal. You can take shortcuts (jelly crystals, pre-made custard, tinned fruit) but I believe making your own fresh components is what creates a very special trifle.

2 plain sponge cakes
2 cups medium dry sherry
3 tablespoons cherry brandy
2 jellies
1 litre pouring custard
600ml pure cream
50g fresh cherries, stones removed
4 pears, peeled and stewed
6 peaches, peeled and stewed
6 apricots, peeled and stewed
plain sponge cake
4 eggs
¾ cup caster sugar
⅔ cup cornflour
¼ cup custard powder
1 teaspoon cream of tartar
½ teaspoon bicarbonate of soda

Port wine jelly

In France during summer there are antique markets (brocantes) in every village and they are great places to find treasures. Last year I found two glass jelly moulds and it has inspired me to make a variety of different 'real' jellies.

2 cups water
1 cup caster sugar
2 tablespoons red currant jelly
zest and juice of two lemons
1 tablespoon powdered gelatine
2 cups red wine
1¼ cups port wine

Mix together the water, sugar, red currant jelly, lemon juice and zest in a heavy-based saucepan and bring to the boil. In a small bowl mix together the gelatine powder and 1 tablespoon of the red wine, to make a paste. Stir this into the hot liquid, continuing to stir with a wire whisk until the gelatine has completely dissolved. Take off the heat. Add the rest of the wine and the port, stir well and refrigerate until set. Serve with good quality vanilla icecream.

cooking time 3 minutes • serves 4

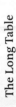

The Long Table

For the sponge cakes, lightly grease and flour two 22cm round cake tins. Whisk together the sugar and eggs until the sugar has dissolved and the mix becomes thick and smooth. The dry ingredients should be sifted three times and folded lightly into the egg mixture using a spatula. Place half the mixture in each cake tin and bake in a preheated oven (180º) for 20 minutes. Cool cakes on a wire rack.

For the homemade jelly, buy packaged gelatin and follow the instructions. I make one port wine jelly and one with blackcurrant juice. Each jelly should be about 400 ml and I use less than a cup of sugar for each one because there are so many other 'sweet' ingredients in the trifle that the jellies don't need to be sickly sweet. For the homemade pouring custard, see Banana Custard page 49.

For the stewed fruit, the pears can be peeled and halved and quartered, with the core removed. Then poached in a sugar syrup (1 cup water to ½ cup sugar) until tender (test with a skewer). The peaches and apricots can be peeled by covering them for 30 seconds with boiling water. The skins should slip off. Then halve and cut into slices that resemble those seen with tinned fruit.

To assemble the trifle, use a large glass or crystal bowl if possible. Cut each sponge cake in half and line the entire bowl with slices of cake. Mix the sherry and cherry brandy together in a jug, and pour some over the cake – don't totally saturate the cake but make sure each slice gets a good slosh of the alcoholic liquid. Now start layering the ingredients inside the bowl. The fruit followed by some scoops of jelly followed by some custard. Top this with another layer of cake and pour on some more sherry and brandy. Keep layering until the bowl has been filled then topped with a deep layer of whipped cream. The fresh, pitted cherries can be used to decorate the top of the trifle, but this should be done at the last moment.

Trifle looks better when served in a glass bowl so that the layers of fruit, custard and jelly can be seen. It's almost a pity to eat it.

Desserts

When we have dessert – which isn't after every meal – it's usually based on whatever is around in the garden at the time. Apples, plums, rhubarb or berry fruits. But sometimes, when the whole family is together, we do 'sheer indulgence' desserts. A celebration rather than a routine.

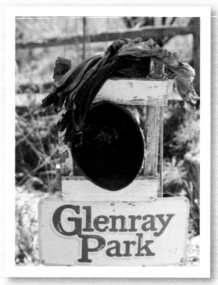

Miriam's white Tiramisu

1 packet pavlova nests (meringues)
2 eggs, separated
90g caster sugar
400g mascarpone
200ml bacardi rum
200ml milk
1 large packet sponge finger biscuits
4 squares rich dark chocolate

This rich dessert looks great in a glass bowl where the layers can be appreciated. A medium-sized bowl, about 10 cm deep, would be ideal. Whisk the egg yolks and sugar together until light and fluffy. Add the mascarpone, a little at a time, until blended. Beat one egg white until it forms peaks. This should then be folded into the mascarpone mixture. In a shallow bowl mix the rum and milk. The idea is to dip the biscuits into this until they are soaked but not crumbly. Start lining the bowl with biscuits – the first layer will be between 8-10 biscuits. Now add a layer of the egg/mascarpone mix – probably about one third of the total, and top this with crumbled meringue – this can be easily done by hand. Now add another layer of biscuits soaked in rum and milk, more egg/mascarpone and more crumbled meringue. You may have enough ingredients for a third layer, topped with the mascarpone cream. Cover and refrigerate for several hours before serving. Miriam likes to gild the lily by grating chocolate on top! The children go wild for this concoction.

Rhubarb and apple crumble

Our neighbour grows wonderful rhubarb and often drops a bunch in our letterbox – we always say the rhubarb fairy has visited. Our apple tree is prolific and the fruits combine to great effect.

1 large bunch rhubarb, washed and chopped
6 large cooking apples, peeled, cored and sliced
4 tablespoons water
⅔ cup of raw sugar
topping
200g unsalted butter, at room temperature
300g plain flour
150g raw sugar

Cook the rhubarb and apple together with the water and sugar, keeping a close watch to ensure it doesn't overcook. Remember that rhubarb is notorious for boiling over (and making a huge mess on the stove) so keep the cooking temperature very low. Allow to cool slightly and put into a shallow, ovenproof dish.
Cut the butter into cubes and rub, one cube at a time, into the flour with your fingers. It should resemble breadcrumbs. Stir in the sugar and spread this mixture over the rhubarb and apple with a small dab of butter. Cook in a moderate oven (180º) for 25-35 minutes until bubbling and brown on top. Allow to cool slightly and serve with whipped cream or pouring custard (see page 49).
cooking time 25-35 minutes • serves 4-6

serves 4

My daughter Miriam is a better cook than me – more like her grandmother in attention to detail. When we all get together she whips up tiramisu in no time.

Our neighbour leaves rhubarb at the letter box once a week in summer.

Food, wine and family –
my favourite way to
spend an afternoon.
Conversation is often
loud and boisterous and
there are seldom any
leftovers, especially
when it comes to dessert.

There's much more to it than just sharing food. We share the joys as well as the trials and tribulations of family life.

Peaches poached in plum syrup

We have both plum and peach trees so this dessert is home gown. The plum syrup I make in spring and bottle for later use. The peaches ripen in summer, and out comes the syrup for poaching.

10 large peaches, peeled and halved
2kg plums
4 cups water
2-3 cups sugar

Wash plums and boil in water for 15-20 minutes. Strain through a fine sieve then return the liquid to the saucepan and add sugar. Simmer for 20 minutes until the syrup has reduced, then pour into clean jars and refrigerate.
Peel the peaches by covering them with boiling water for 1 minute. The skins should slip off easily. Cut in half and arrange, cut side down, in a shallow saucepan, pouring over about 3 cups of syrup. Simmer until the peaches are tender and serve warm with whipped cream.
cooking time 40 minutes • serves 4-6

Lemon delicious pudding

This is the lightest pudding imaginable, with a tangy lemon sauce at the bottom that is spooned over the cake. Because it must be cooked and eaten immediately, it needs to go into the oven while you are sitting down to the main course – a bit of a juggling act but well worth it.

3 eggs, separated
½ cup caster sugar
1 cup milk
1 tablespoon self-raising flour, sifted
3 lemons, juiced
zest of two lemons
1 tablespoon caster sugar

Mix together the egg yolks and sugar, beating until they become creamy and thick. Mix in the milk, flour, lemon juice and zest and beat thoroughly. Whisk the egg whites until they form peaks, gradually adding the caster sugar. Fold the eggs whites into the lemon mixture and pour into a greased pudding bowl. This should be placed in a water bath (a baking dish half filled with tepid water) and cooked in a moderate (175°) oven for 50-60 minutes.
cooking time 50-60 minutes • serves 4

Index

Recipe index

Conversion chart

measures

One Australian metric measuring cup holds approximately 250ml; one Australian metric tablespoon holds 20ml; one Australian metric teaspoon holds 5ml.

The difference between one country's measuring cups and another's is within a two- or three-teaspoon variance, and will not affect your cooking results. North America, New Zealand and the United Kingdom use a 15ml tablespoon.

All cup and spoon measurements are level. The most accurate way of measuring dry ingredients is to weigh them. When measuring liquids, use a clear glass or plastic jug with the metric markings.

We use large eggs with an average weight of 60g.

dry measures

metric	imperial
15g	½oz
30g	1oz
60g	2oz
90g	3oz
125g	4oz (¼lb)
155g	5oz
185g	6oz
220g	7oz
250g	8oz (½lb)
280g	9oz
315g	10oz
345g	11oz
375g	12oz (¾lb)
410g	13oz
440g	14oz
470g	15oz
500g	16oz (1lb)
750g	24oz (1½lb)
1kg	32oz (2lb)

liquid measures

metric	imperial
30ml	1 fluid oz
60ml	2 fluid oz
100ml	3 fluid oz
125ml	4 fluid oz
150ml	5 fluid oz (¼ pint/1 gill)
190ml	6 fluid oz
250ml	8 fluid oz
300ml	10 fluid oz (½ pint)
500ml	16 fluid oz
600ml	20 fluid oz (1 pint)
1000ml (1 litre)	1¾ pints

length measures

metric	imperial
3mm	⅛ in
6mm	¼in
1cm	½in
2cm	¾in
2.5cm	1in
5cm	2in
6cm	2½in
8cm	3in
10cm	4in
13cm	5in
15cm	6in
18cm	7in
20cm	8in
23cm	9in
25cm	10in
28cm	11in
30cm	12in (1ft)

oven temperatures

These oven temperatures are only a guide for conventional ovens. For fan-forced ovens, check the manufacturer's manual.

	°C (Celsius)	°F (Fahrenheit)	Gas Mark
Very slow	120	250	½
Slow	150	275-300	1-2
Moderately slow	160	325	3
Moderate	180	350-375	4-5
Moderately hot	200	400	6
Hot	220	425-450	7-8
Very hot	240	475	9

Acknowledgments There are many people to thank for helping create this book. My mother, of course, for bothering to teach me to cook in the first place. My husband David for clearing the table and washing up for several decades. My children and their partners for their appreciation of our boisterous family gatherings. My grandchildren for their sheer enjoyment of food (well, maybe not Ella and Isabella who are picky!). A special thanks to Simone for helping chop, slice and cook for the photography. And my dear friend Nadja La Ganza for her photographic artistry and passion for the project. My agent Lyn Tranter for keeping the idea going, my publisher Christine Whiston for her faith that it would be rewarding, and the team at ACP Books. Lastly, all our dear friends and family who have come to the table. It was always a pleasure. *Mary Moody*

The publishers have made every effort to gain permission for the use of copyright material in this book.

General manager *Christine Whiston*
Editorial director *Susan Tomnay*
Creative director & designer *Hieu Chi Nguyen*
Editor *Sarah Plant*
Photographer (studio) *Tanya Zouev*
Stylist (studio) *Janet Mitchell*
Food prep (studio) *Cassandra Stokes*
Photographer (location) *Simon Griffiths*
Stylist (location) *Megan Morton*
Food prep (location) *Cassandra Stokes*
Photographer (France) *Nadja La Ganza*

Director of sales *Brian Cearnes*
Marketing manager *Bridget Cody*
Business analyst *Ashley Davies*
Operations manager *David Scotto*
International rights enquiries *Laura Bamford*
lbamford@acpuk.com

ACP Books are published by ACP Magazines
a division of PBL Media Pty Limited
Group publisher, Women's lifestyle *Pat Ingram*
Director of sales, Women's lifestyle *Lynette Phillips*
Commercial manager, Women's lifestyle *Seymour Cohen*
Marketing director, Women's lifestyle *Matthew Dominello*
Public relations manager, Women's lifestyle *Hannah Deveraux*
Creative director, Events, Women's lifestyle *Luke Bonnano*
Research Director, Women's lifestyle *Justin Stone*
ACP Magazines, Chief Executive officer *Scott Lorson*
PBL Media, Chief Executive officer *Ian Law*

The publishers would like to thank the following people for props used in photography *Margaret Tate, Yvonne van Dyke, Beverley Griffiths*
Photograph on pp46-47 of apples *Joshua Dasey*
Photograph on pp28-29 of Balmoral Beach
Frederick Charles Saxon,
Mosman Library Local Studies Collection

Produced by ACP Books, Sydney.
Published by ACP Books, a division of ACP Magazines Ltd.
54 Park St, Sydney NSW Australia 2000. GPO Box 4088, Sydney, NSW 2001.
Phone +61 2 9282 8618 Fax +61 2 9267 9438
acpbooks@acpmagazines.com.au www.acpbooks.com.au
Printed by C&C Offset Printing, China.
Australia Distributed by Network Services, GPO Box 4088, Sydney, NSW 2001.
Phone +61 2 9282 8777 Fax +61 2 9264 3278
networkweb@networkservicescompany.com.au
United Kingdom Distributed by Australian Consolidated Press (UK),
10 Scirocco Close, Moulton Park Office Village, Northampton, NN3 6AP.
Phone +44 1604 642 200 Fax +44 1604 642 300
books@acpuk.com www.acpuk.com
New Zealand Distributed by Netlink Distribution Company, ACP Media Centre,
Cnr Fanshawe and Beaumont Streets, Westhaven, Auckland.
PO Box 47906, Ponsonby, Auckland, NZ.
Phone +64 9 366 9966 Fax 0800 277 412 ask@ndc.co.nz
South Africa Distributed by PSD Promotions, 30 Diesel Road Isando, Gauteng
Johannesburg. PO Box 1175, Isando 1600, Gauteng Johannesburg.
Phone +27 11 392 6065/6/7 Fax +27 11 392 6079/80 orders@psdprom.co.za
Canada Distributed by Publishers Group Canada Order Desk & Customer Service
9050 Shaughnessy Street, Vancouver, BC V6P 6E5 Phone (800) 663 5714
Fax (800) 565 3770 service@raincoast.com

Author: Moody, Mary, 1950–
Title: The long table/author, Mary Moody.
Publisher: Sydney: ACP Books, 2008.
ISBN: 978-1-86396-773-0 (hbk)
Notes: Includes index.
Subjects: Cookery.
Dewey Number: 641.5
Copyright © ACP Magazines Ltd 2008 ABN 18 053 273 546
Photography copyright © ACP Magazines Ltd; Mary Moody
Text copyright © Mary Moody

To order books, phone 136 116 (within Australia).
Send recipe enquiries to: recipeenquiries@acpmagazines.com.au